FOR BREW
FREAKS,
BEAN
GEEKS,
AND
THE
SIMPLY
CURIOUS ...

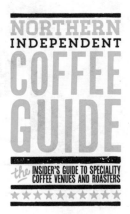

NORTHERN
INDEPENDENT
COFFEE
GUIDE

the INSIDER'S GUIDE TO SPECIALITY
COFFEE VENUES AND ROASTERS

★★★★★★★★★★★

Nº2

Salt Media, 5 Cross Street, Devon, EX31 1BA.
www.saltmedia.co.uk
Tel: 01271 859299
Email: ideas@saltmedia.co.uk

Salt Media *Independent Coffee Guide* team:
Nick Cooper, Catherine Jones, Kathryn Lewis,
Charley Pope, Tamsin Powell, Jo Rees, Chris Sheppard,
Dale Stiling, Mark Tibbles, Amy Mae-Turner and Holly West.
Design and illustration: Salt Media

**A big thank you to the *Independent Coffee Guide*
committee** (meet them on page 180) for their expertise
and enthusiasm, **our headline sponsors** Schluter
and Cimbali, **and sponsors** Beyond the Bean, Bunn,
Cakesmiths, Cup North, J. Atkinson & Co., SCAE
and Yeo Valley.

Coffee shops, cafes and roasters are invited to be
included in the guide based on meeting criteria set by
our committee, which includes a high quality coffee
experience for visitors, use of speciality beans and
being independently run.

For information on the Northern, South West and
Scottish *Independent Coffee Guides*, visit:
www.indycoffee.guide

🐦 @indycoffeeguide
📷 @indycoffeeguide

Welcome to the second edition of the *Northern Independent Coffee Guide*.

Since we launched the first northern edition of the guide a year ago, new indie cafes and roasteries have popped up all over the place, spreading the word about speciality coffee and creating converts.

As a consequence, this year's book is significantly bigger and includes more finds for a seriously good caffeine fix.

We've seen lots of developments over the last year as bean seasonality has become more widely recognised, and new and exciting harvests from micro-lots have been sourced and roasted.

'THIS YEAR'S GUIDE INCLUDES EVEN MORE FINDS FOR A SERIOUSLY GOOD CAFFEINE FIX'

In the cafes, brew bars are booming, coffee tonics are having a moment, and we've seen more batch brewing and guest roasts, along with innovative food to accompany the drinks.

So it's a great moment to be a coffee fan, and we've had fun travelling around, checking out what's going on and meeting lovely people who are passionate about the bean.

A huge thanks goes out to our coffee guide committee for their input and creative energies (meet them on page 180) and also to our headline sponsors Cimbali and Schluter, and sponsors Beyond the Bean, Bunn, Cakesmiths, Cup North, J. Atkinson & Co., SCAE and Yeo Valley who all help make the guide happen.

Jo Rees
Editor
🐦 @indycoffeeguide

CONTENTS

12	WELCOME	156	COFFEE GLOSSARY
14	THE GOLDEN AGE OF STEAM	160	INDEX
19	INDY COFFEE GUIDE DINER MUG	166	MAPS
20	TECHNO-LOGICAL COFFEE	168	NEWCASTLE MAP
24	BEGINNER'S GUIDE TO BEANS	169	LIVERPOOL MAP
29	CUP NORTH	170	MANCHESTER MAP
30	YOUR JOURNEY STARTS HERE	171	YORK MAP
		172	LEEDS MAP
32	VENUES	173	SHEFFIELD MAP
34	TYNE AND WEAR & SURROUNDS	175	NORTH OF ENGLAND MAP
42	CUMBRIA, LANCASHIRE & MERSEYSIDE	180	MEET THE COMMITTEE
62	GREATER MANCHESTER & CHESHIRE		
76	NORTH & WEST YORKSHIRE		
106	SOUTH YORKSHIRE & LINCOLNSHIRE		
118	MORE GOOD CUPS		
122	ROASTERS		
154	MORE GOOD ROASTERS		

The independent speciality coffee sector is still growing at a staggering rate and this year's guide to the northern scene reflects this

The first change you'll notice is that we've included an important word in the guide's title this year: "speciality". It's important to us for many reasons. Speciality is, first and foremost, the highest grade of coffee – just six per cent of the global harvest – and represents all the close attention to detail right through the long coffee supply chain, from hand picking the cherries to the brewing and flavour extraction.

'SPECIALITY COFFEE REPRESENTS JUST 6 PER CENT OF THE GLOBAL HARVEST'

I love to see the myriad of individual interpretations of the speciality coffee offering from both roasters and cafes. As roasters we talk about the terroir of the coffee as one of the contributing factors that create the distinctive flavour profiles in the cup. And your local independent cafe also contributes to the terroir of its neighbourhood, providing local colour and identity in communities where the high street is in danger of being yet another clone.

As the independent market matures, we'll see even more mutations and creative interpretation of the cafe space. To avoid us becoming a chain of independents, we need to focus on our individuality and enjoy the benefits of small scale

decision-making that gives us the agility to adopt new ideas quickly.

The speciality coffee world is full of career epiphanists who, like me, have jumped ship from a previous life and are intent on enjoying the roller coaster ride that we find ourselves on. It's a world that emphasises collaboration over competition, a sense of us all being in it together, aware of our place providing a connection between the producer and the consumer.

The guide is an attempt to curate this movement in our region, so that you too can experience some of the enthusiasm and effort that goes into making that cup of coffee.

It's not all soul searching and serious though, you'll discover some brilliant places and people having fun with the format. And with an ever-increasing variety to choose from, we hope to lead you to some exciting speciality coffee discoveries in the North.

Ian Steel
Proprietor, J. Atkinson & Co.
Northern guide committee member

🐦 @coffeehopper

THE GOLDEN AGE OF STEAM

Robert Ward of Cimbali journeys through the history of the coffee machine, and reveals some photographic gems from the archive

There is an element of pride as to who first created espresso and espresso machines, as well as differing opinions on the meaning of the name. Folklore gets bandied around the industry, so this is my take on things ...

FRENCH BEGINNINGS?

There are indications that it was actually the French who created the first espresso, using steam to push water through coffee to create a pressurised brew. In 1818 a Mr Laurens of Paris used a percolator system to create coffee and in 1822 there were further improvements by Louis Bernard Rabaut.

But the first, more recognisable espresso machine was built by Luigi Bezzera in 1901. It was the more recognisable Belle Epoque column-style machine that was very popular in the early 1900s - some people still like the impressive towers today and have lovingly recreated them.

ENTER CIMBALI

Cimbali came along quite early in espresso history, in 1912. The company was predated by only a few that are still around today, like Victoria Arduino (owned by Nuova Simonelli) and La Pavoni. Others followed later on such as La Marzocco in 1927, Nuova Simonelli in 1936, Gaggia in 1938, FAEMA (Factory Electro Mechanical and Associated Equipment) in 1945 and La Spaziale in 1969.

The main ways in which coffee machines have developed over time have been the small improvements in how we heat and control the water. This started off with wood and coal burning units, moving on to gas and electricity in later years.

In the early days, controlling the boiler pressure was done with various lead weights on top of a small steam valve, which was followed by spring valves and the much more sophisticated, electronically-controlled steam valves.

BIRTH OF THE CREMA

The most significant developments in modern espresso came between 1938-1945 when Achille Gaggia created the first steam-free espresso, using a piston and lever to create pressure with a more controlled water temperature. He created the first crema caffè which was when the modern expectation of consistent foam-topped coffee was born.

In the 1950s, La Cimbali experimented with a hydraulic system to generate the pressure needed for espresso without the need for the barista to have to physically exert force with a manual lever.

ENTER THE E61

In the late fifties FAEMA started working on a system which it released in 1961. The E61 was the first machine to use a volumetric pump to push the water onto the coffee cake at a pressure of nine atmospheres (which was needed to produce the espresso), which replaced the requirement for the lever.

The E61 also introduced the pre-infusion principle, where wetting the ground coffee for a few seconds first, provides the maximum extraction of aromatic substances. This took espresso production to a completely new level in terms of flavour characteristics and consistency, and revolutionised machine design.

To this day, the pre-infusion group head of that machine is one of the most copied in the espresso machine world.

Left: Cimbali machines through the ages

FINE TUNING

Throughout the 1980s and 1990s, there was more experimentation with temperature control and ever increasing demands for stability to suit those more delicate – and less forgiving – coffees. That work continues to this day in our modern era of pressure and temperature profiling machines.

A machine like the M100 can adjust individual boiler temperature and pressure profiles at the press of a few buttons, which gives the serious coffee geek ultimate control. It means that developing single origin espresso and delicate roast profiles has never been more accessible.

'THE FIRST CREMA CAFFÈ WAS WHEN THE MODERN EXPECTATION OF CONSISTENT FOAM-TOPPED COFFEE WAS BORN'

SCHLUTER

WE BELIEVE
IN THE
FUTURE OF
AFRICA

INDY COFFEE GUIDE
DINER MUG

If you're drinking top quality beans at home, you'll want to slurp it from something equally special

We've sourced just 30 of the most solid, chunky diner mugs direct from the US and decorated them with our hand crafted 'stay casual' sloth coffee illustration by artist Jose Walker.

It's guaranteed to keep your coffee warm while looking pretty cool. Order yours, priced £9.99 from the website.

WWW.INDYCOFFEE.GUIDE

'IMAGINE IF
YOU COULD TIP
A FARMER IN
AFRICA WHILE
DRINKING HIS
COFFEE'

TECHNO-LOGICAL COFFEE

'We've entered the 4th wave of the coffee revolution,' says Liverpool-based green bean importer, Phil Schluter. 'It's hard to determine when a ripple becomes a wave, but one thing is for sure, technology is changing the industry at an ever-increasing pace – and it's an exhilarating place to be'

The coffee industry has the potential to be a major driver for economic change in the communities which produce coffee, so it's exciting to see technology at the forefront of innovation in the industry, because it offers the ability to affect real change.

PAYMENT BY MOBILE MONEY

On a recent trip to East Africa, I was talking to suppliers who are now paying farmers using mobile money. One big issue among farming communities is the lack of banking services, and thus the inability to store or save money.

For example, in Ethiopia, most farmers have no way of storing money or value other than keeping cherries in their hut. Mobile money overcomes this obstacle. It also offers a new way to track farmer payments, and build the vital economic transparency into a supply chain.

IKAWA DIGITAL ROASTER

I've been involved in developing the Ikawa portable coffee roaster, and remain on the board of directors. It's exciting to see technology which enables coffee to be roasted at source.

Empowering farmers to taste what they produce will help them identify how to improve quality, and fight for a higher price for the better cupping lots.

The Pro Sample Roaster provides the chance to create a common language for sample roasting, by sharing roast profiles digitally, which enables more informed discussions on coffee flavour through the supply chain – from origin to roaster.

'IT ALLOWS COFFEE TO BE ROASTED AT SOURCE, SO FARMERS CAN TASTE THEIR OWN PRODUCT'

OPEN DATA

I recently spent a fascinating day in The Hague discussing the potential to use open data platforms to bring coffee consumers and coffee producers together. Imagine if you could tip a farmer in Africa while drinking his coffee. Imagine if your mobile allowed you to tip your barista and your farmer at the touch of a screen. In an industry where many farmers in East Africa still live on $2-3 per day, this could revolutionise their lives.

GIS MAPPING

Our Virunga project in the Democratic Republic of Congo (DRC), now has 1800 farms that are certified organic.

We've used inexpensive GIS software to map the farms and can log into Google Earth to locate each one of them. Production levels mean that it is still a challenge to offer farmer-specific lots from DRC, but the transparency and traceability is already in place to provide them in the future. We hope that with improved agronomy through the training we provide, and better prices, volumes will increase, allowing for farmer-specific lots of sufficient size to be offered to buyers around the world.

These are just a few ways in which technology brings power to those who have it, and there are many other innovations across the sector. It's important that technology is deployed to the benefit of those who need it most in the supply chain, connecting farmers to the international markets and helping them gain better value for their great coffees.

'WE'VE USED INEXPENSIVE GIS SOFTWARE TO MAP THE FARMS'

BEGINNER'S GUIDE TO BEANS

Find yourself skimming over terms such as washed, natural and robusta and skipping straight to the tasting notes when searching out a new brew? We asked Paul Meikle-Janney of Dark Woods to give us the lowdown on the mighty bean and help clear up any confusing coffee spiel

1. SPECIES

With just a couple of species of coffee bean commonly available, you'd think deciphering between the two would be easy, but nothing is simple when it comes to speciality coffee.

More than 65 per cent of the coffee sold around the world is made from arabica beans, with the remainder predominantly made up of robusta. *'Arabica is seen as the premium choice,'* explains Paul, *'it has a cleaner taste, with more fruity, acidic and floral flavours. Robusta, on the other hand, has a more bitter finish and a richer, round body.'*

There are also loads of different varieties of arabica (and robusta) too, such as bourbon, typica, geisha and caturra.

With tasting notes on the opposite sides of the spectrum, you'll often find the two bean species blended together to produce a smooth, Italian style espresso.

ROBUSTA 30%

ARABICA+ 65%

LATIN

AFRICA

2. ORIGIN

In the same way that the terroir of a region: soil, climate and altitude, impact upon wine production, it also affects the flavour of the coffee bean. '*Of course*,' says Paul, '*coffee growing regions can't all be bundled into the same bag, but here are a few general pointers.*'

CENTRAL AMERICA
Acidic and fruity notes are prominent in good quality Central beans.

ETHIOPIA
The east offers wine and blueberry flavours, while the west is known for its jasmine scented florals.

INDIA
Famous for its robusta, with a clean and sweeter taste.

SOUTH AMERICA
Expect wheaty, nutty flavours with a sweet and mellow finish.

KENYA
This region has been known for blackcurrant tasting notes but fresh, acidic flavours such as lemon tea are more common.

INDONESIA
Lower acidity and a fuller body produces rich, chocolate flavours.

3. PROCESSING

Once the coffee cherries have been picked, the seed (bean) inside needs to be removed.

There are two main ways of doing this - washed or natural - with each method creating a distinct flavour. *'For washed coffees, the beans are squeezed from the ripe fruit then washed to remove the sticky residue, holding on to all of the citrusy flavours and creating a lighter body,'* explains Paul. *'But in natural coffees, the cherry is dried first before the beans are separated from the brittle skins, resulting in a sweeter taste and lower acidity.'*

... AND SQUEEZE!

'A SHORTER SPELL IN THE ROASTER YIELDS NATURAL ACIDIC AND FRUITY FLAVOURS WITH LESS BITTERNESS'

ROASTY TOASTY!

4. ROASTING

Light or dark, the roast is probably the part of the coffee producing chain you're most familiar with. Light roasts are synonymous with the recent speciality boom: *'a shorter spell in the roaster yields natural acidic and fruity flavours with less bitterness,'* says Paul. *'In darker roasts, the majority of the acidity is burnt off, producing caramel roast flavours and eventually, a bitter taste.'*

CALLING ALL MILK-LOVERS

Wherever you buy our milk, rest assured we always pay our farmers a fair price for it. We've worked with some of them for over 20 years and, as farmers ourselves, we know everyone needs to make a living.

OUR MILK WILL ALWAYS:

✓ Come from our farm or The Organic Milk Suppliers Cooperative

✓ Come from cows fed on a pesticide and GM-free diet

✓ Come exclusively from British farms

✓ Taste great, the right way

FIND OUT MORE AT:
YEOVALLEY.CO.UK/MILKLOVERS

Yeo valley
FAMILY FARM

CUP NORTH

NOVEMBER 5-6, 2016

The North's fave coffee festival returns in 2016 with two days of fully caffeinated adventures at its new venue, Victoria Warehouse in Manchester.

In addition to stands and demos from leading coffee companies, visitors can watch (and get involved in) the UK Coffee Throwing Championships, SCAE UK competitions, check out the Cupping Zone, and explore a world of tea and hot chocolate specialists.

Cup North organiser Hannah Davies says, *'We're really excited about holding the event in a bigger venue as it means we can have more exhibitors, live music and a Coffee/Craft Workshop Zone. Look out too for the new format Tamper Tantrum'*.

See you there.

www.cupnorth.co.uk

YOUR JOURNEY STARTS HERE

VENUES

These are coffee shops and cafes where you can drink top notch speciality coffee. We've split the whole of the north of England into areas to help you find places near you.

ROASTERS

Meet the leading speciality coffee roasters in the North and discover where to source beans to use at home.

Finally, you'll discover More Good Cups and More Good Roasters at the end of each section. These are businesses who also make the grade.

MAPS

Every venue and roaster has a number so you can find them either on the large fold-out map or the detailed city maps – all at the back of the guide.

Don't forget to let us know how you get on as you explore the North's best speciality coffee venues and roasters:

🐦 @indycoffeeguide 📷 @indycoffeeguide www.indycoffee.guide

MARMADUKES COFFEE

ROASTED FOR ESPRESSO
CULT OF DONE V.20
WORKSHOP COFFEE CO.
RWANDA

ROASTED FOR FILTER
FINCA LAS PAVAS
WORKSHOP COFFEE CO.
WASHED PROCESS
COLOMBIA

POUR OVER
(KALITA WAVE)
OR AEROPRESS

TEA
YORKSHIRE TEA   4.0
WITH REFILL
BIG POT   4.2

JOE'S TEA   4.0
THE EARL OF GREY
PROPER PEPPERMINT
MINTED UP FRUIT
WHITER THAN WHITE
SWEET CHAMOMILE
ST.CLEMENT'S LEMON
QUEEN OF GREEN
BERRY BEST

ESPRESSO	2.1
AMERICANO	2.5
FLAT WHITE	2.6
CAPPUCCINO	2.6
LATTE	2.6
MOCHA	3.0
CORTADO	2.4
MACCHIATO	2.4

ICED
LATTE   2.8
MOCHA   3.0
COLD BREW   3.0

HOT CHOC
SINGLE ORIGIN   2.8
CLASSIC 70% OR WHITE
WHM... etc   2.8

BONSOY MILK 0.4 EXTRA

16ᵗʰ MARCH:
BREW WORKSHOP:
POUR OVERS/
V60

20

VENUES

TYNE AND WEAR
& SURROUNDS

MAP N° 1. BLK COFFEE

214 Chillingham Road, Heaton, Newcastle upon Tyne, NE6 5LP.

BLK may be one of the North's newest speciality spots, but with seasoned barista Alison Bell behind the sleek Heaton hangout, this is no new kid on the coffee block.

Placing second in the 2016 UK Brewers Cup, Alison knows her stuff, so it's no surprise to find an impressive range of brewing methods and a hefty selection of beans to choose from at her first solo venture.

INSIDER'S TIP — LOOK OUT FOR COFFEE CLASSES COMING SOON

As a multi-roaster shop, the line-up of coffees available to drink is constantly evolving, but don't despair if you're a fresher at all this coffee geekery, Alison and her friendly baristas are on hand with unpretentious advice. There's also a handy clipboard complete with sketches to explain each brew method.

The clean and contemporary interior complements the modern approach to coffee without being cold or unapproachable. So pull up one of the metal stools and treat yourself to a quirky bake - the crack pie, a croissant-doughnut pastry mashup, is a must - or grab a coffee to go if it's packed out with punters.

KEY ROASTERS
Workshop Coffee, Five Elephant

BREWING METHODS
Espresso, Chemex, AeroPress, french press, Kalita Wave, V60, cold drip

MACHINE
La Marzocco Linea Classic MP

GRINDERS
Mythos One, Mazzer Super Jolly, Baratza Forte

OPENING HOURS
Mon-Fri 7am-6pm
Sat 8am-5pm
Sun 9am-4pm

 Gluten FREE

 COFFEE BEANS AVAILABLE

 SOYA MILK AVAILABLE

 WIFI

 CYCLE FRIENDLY

 OUTDOOR SEATING

 COFFEE COURSES AVAILABLE

 FAMILY FRIENDLY

 DISABLED ACCESS

 DOG FRIENDLY

T: 07595 493488

f BLK Coffee   @blkcoffeeheaton   @blkcoffeeheaton

№2. HARVEST

91 St Georges Terrace, Jesmond, Newcastle upon Tyne, NE2 2DN.

The original canteen from Ouseburn Coffee Co., Harvest is a mile outside Newcastle city centre in Jesmond, and worth tracking down for its laid back atmosphere, minimalist styling, great coffee (from its own roastery, naturally) and lovely food.

The all-day breakfast and brunch is a massive hit with the regulars, especially the poached eggs with smoked salmon and avocado smash.

Choose espresso-based drinks as well as coffee through the AeroPress and V60, or on hot days join the throng drinking OCC's new cold brew – not to be confused with your regular iced coffee.

Now open in the evenings, Harvest regularly hosts special events such as poetry readings, book clubs, supper clubs and speakeasy-style cocktail nights, so you can indulge your passion for good coffee with lots of creative delights on the side.

KEY ROASTER
Ouseburn Coffee Co.

BREWING METHODS
Espresso, V60, AeroPress, cold brew

MACHINE
Linea PB

GRINDER
Mahlkonig EK40

OPENING HOURS
Mon-Sun
8am-10pm

INSIDER'S TIP
CHOOSE ANY OCC COFFEE BEANS FOR YOUR DRINK

www.ouseburncoffee.co.uk   T: 07572 138729

f Ouseburn Coffee   🐦 @ouseburncoffee   📷 @ousebourncoffee

№3. FLAT CAPS COFFEE

13 Ridley Place, Newcastle upon Tyne, NE1 8JQ.

Good things come in threes at Flat Caps Coffee on Ridley Place. Firstly there's the man behind Newcastle's pocket-sized caffeine bunker: three time northern barista champ, Joe Meagher.

Then there's his offering of at least three different guest coffees at any time – available as espresso or brew bar – with up to fifteen to choose from during special events such as the cafe's popular Paris Coffee Week shenanigans.

INSIDER'S TIP TRY THE HOMEMADE COLD DRIP WITH TONIC WATER

And finally, there are the three brew methods on offer: Kalita Wave, AeroPress and syphon, through which you can trial Joe's latest choices from an ever expanding list of indie roasters.

And that's not even counting the coffee tasting flights, impressive selection of loose leaf teas or tasty lunch offerings.

KEY ROASTER
Workshop Coffee

BREWING METHODS
Espresso,
Kalita Wave,
AeroPress, syphon,
cold drip

MACHINE
Sanremo Verona

GRINDERS
Mahlkonig K30,
Mahlkonig EK43

OPENING HOURS
Mon-Sat
10am-5.30pm

 Gluten FREE

 COFFEE BEANS AVAILABLE

 SOYA MILK AVAILABLE

 WIFI

 DOG FRIENDLY

www.flatcapscoffee.com T: 01912 327836

f Flat Caps Coffee   @flatcapjoe   @flatcapjoe

MAP.4. FENWICK FOODHALL

39 Northumberland Street, Newcastle upon Tyne, NE1 7AS.

When Fenwick unveiled the multimillion pound refurb of its Foodhall in the summer of 2015, there was a lot of excitement about the wine shop, seafood and oyster bar, and South East Asian street food concept. But what speciality coffee fans were salivating over was the chance to drink and buy Ouseburn Coffee at yet another outlet in the city.

The much loved coffee company - and first indie roasters in the city - has taken its flair to the Foodhall with a Nitro brew bar and freshly roasted coffee, bagged and ground to order.

INSIDER'S TIP **RETURN YOUR RECYCLED COLD BREW BOTTLES FOR DISCOUNTS AND REWARDS**

As all the coffee at OCC's local roastery is cooked up in small batches, it's as fresh as can be, and by selling the beans by the gram, there's an opportunity to try as many varieties as possible.

In addition to espresso-based classics to drink in or take out, uniquely, there's also a choice of Nitro coffee on tap, espresso martinis and cold brew made with a delicate, fruity single origin Ethiopian coffee, which has been slow brewed for 20 hours and triple filtered.

KEY ROASTER
Ouseburn Coffee Co.

BREWING METHODS
Espresso, Nitro, cold brew

MACHINE
Linea PB

GRINDER
Mahlkonig EK40

OPENING HOURS
Mon-Fri 9am-8pm
Sat 9am-7pm
Sun 11am-5pm

www.ouseburncoffee.co.uk T: 07572 138729

f Ouseburn Coffee   🐦 @ouseburncoffee   📷 @ouseburncoffee

5. FLAT WHITE KITCHEN

40 Saddler Street, Durham, DH1 3NU.

There's some serious brunchin' business going down at Flat White Kitchen and if you're a buttermilk pancakes, all-day-eggs, sourdough toast kinda' person, you'll want to get in on the action.

Just a hop, skip and a jump away from Durham Cathedral, the refurbished 16th century town house has been restored to its former glory and treated to a 21st century revamp with copper pipes, stripped wood and opulent mirrors – interior inspo at its finest.

INSIDER'S TIP OVER DONE IT AT BREAKFAST? COME BACK FOR LUNCH AND EQUAL THINGS OUT WITH THE RAINBOW SUPERFOOD SALAD

Catching the speciality bug in Australia, owners Peter Anglesea and Patrick Clark opened their first caffeinated venture, Flat White Cafe, down the road five years ago and you'll still find them pulling shots and sharing their considerable knowledge with the select baristas who make the cut.

With a knockout team of hand-picked chefs crafting Flat White's menus, the quality and thought behind the food matches the attention paid to the liquid offerings, making this a find.

KEY ROASTER
Ouseburn Coffee Co.

BREWING METHODS
Espresso, pourover, filter

MACHINE
La Marzocco Linea PB 3 Group

GRINDER
Mazzer Robur

OPENING HOURS
Mon-Sat 9am-5pm
Sun 10am-4pm

 Gluten FREE

 COFFEE BEANS AVAILABLE

 SOYA MILK AVAILABLE

 WIFI

 CYCLE FRIENDLY

 OUTDOOR seating

 COFFEE COURSES AVAILABLE

FAMILY FRIENDLY

 DISABLED ACCESS

www.flatwhitedurham.co.uk   T: 07789 951149
f Flat White Kitchen   @flatwhitedurham   @flatwhitedurham

6. BEDFORD ST COFFEE

27 Bedford Street, Middlesbrough, North Yorkshire, TS1 2LL.

A coffee lover's haven in the heart of Middlesbrough, Bedford St Coffee is the first cafe to be opened by the team behind Rounton Coffee.

Offering a delightful alternative to the coffee chains, the focus here is strictly on quality, with every single bean from fully traceable, sustainable sources.

The cafe was partly funded by a successful crowdfunding campaign with hundreds of Rounton Coffee fans pitching in to raise £10,000 to kit out the building.

INSIDER'S TIP GRAB A BAG OF FRESHLY ROASTED ROUNTON BEANS WHILE YOU'RE VISITING

The result is a stylish space, whether you choose to sit in the cosy sofa area at the back of the shop, at a window seat watching the world go by, or to spread out and work at one of the tables.

In addition to delicious cakes and bakes - with a wide range of gluten-free options available - Bedford St Coffee's food menu is all about the mighty bagel. Get 'em stuffed with locally-sourced ingredients such as smoked salmon with cream cheese, lemon and dill, or dry cured beef with horseradish crème fraîche and watercress.

KEY ROASTER
Rounton Coffee

BREWING METHODS
V60, AeroPress

MACHINE
Sanremo Verona RS

GRINDERS
Mahlkonig K30,
Mahlkonig EK43

OPENING HOURS
Mon-Sat 8am-6pm
Sun 10am-4pm

www.rountoncoffee.co.uk   T: 01642 647856

f Bedford St Coffee   @bedfordstcoffee   @bedfordstcoffee

№7. MINT HOBO

30 High Street, Yarm, Stockton on Tees, County Durham, TS15 9AE.

The fabulously-named Mint Hobo is the result of Claire and Steve Ashman's dream of bringing speciality coffee to their High Street in Yarm.

As well as serving delicious coffee that's been exclusively roasted and blended by local micro-roastery Rounton (and brewed by an all-female team of five superstar baristas), you'll find freshly-made juices, smoothies, speciality hot chocolate and a unique blend of Mint Hobo tea.

INSIDER'S TIP SCONE VARIETIES CHANGE DAILY - IT'S DECIDED BY THE MEMBER OF STAFF WHO GETS TO WORK FIRST

On the foodie front, cakes, cookies and scones accompany a range of toasties and panini - the content of which changes daily. And look out for more unusual options on Thursdays when the Hobo team like to experiment. Recent specials include The Elvis, a hip swivelling mash-up of peanut butter, bacon, banana and honey.

Visit too for the regular coffee tasting evenings, which are a great way to kick start your speciality coffee knowledge.

The coffee house is fully licensed from 10am so you can also enjoy a tipple at this friendly venue.

KEY ROASTER
Rounton Coffee

BREWING METHODS
Espresso, percolated, AeroPress, Chemex

MACHINE
Sanremo Opera

GRINDERS
Mahlkonig EK43, Markibar Aspe

OPENING HOURS
Mon-Thu 7am-7pm
Fri-Sat 7am-10pm
Sun 9am-5pm

Gluten FREE

COFFEE BEANS AVAILABLE

SOYA MILK AVAILABLE

WIFI

CYCLE FRIENDLY

OUTDOOR SEATING

COFFEE COURSES AVAILABLE

FAMILY FRIENDLY

DOG FRIENDLY

www.minthobo.co.uk   T: 07763 895806

f Mint Hobo   🐦 @minthobo   📷 @minthobo

CUMBRIA,
LANCASHIRE
& MERSEYSIDE

№8. COFFEE GENIUS

20-21 St Cuthbert's Lane, Carlisle, Cumbria, CA3 8AG.

There's a comprehensive selection of brew methods and a rotating range of seasonal blends to keep the caffeine tourists coming, as well as fuelling locals' obsessions at Coffee Genius in Carlisle.

INSIDER'S TIP WITH A FULLY LICENSED BAR ITS WORTH STICKING AROUND AFTER HOURS

First opening the doors in March 2014, Mike and Lynn Steadman wanted to give the people of this Cumbrian city more choice when it came to coffee, and with six methods showcased at the brew bar and three different single origins, alongside the house espresso blend, it looks like they've gone and done it.

The quality of the coffee crafted from speciality beans is maintained by Coffee Genius' team of highly skilled baristas who are always eager to improve their skills. If you're lucky, you may be pulled in on some taste-testing on a quiet afternoon.

Good coffee deserves good cake, and this airy cafe isn't short of a few homemade delights. We'd recommend the cappuccino cheesecake AND the passion fruit and lime pavlova.

KEY ROASTER
Carvetii

BREWING METHODS
Espresso, V60, AeroPress, Chemex, syphon, french press, filter

MACHINE
La Marzocco FB80

GRINDERS
Mahlkonig K30, Tanzania, Mazzer Mini

OPENING HOURS
Mon-Sat 8.30am-5pm
Sun 10am-4pm

www.coffeegenius.co.uk T: 01228 546594

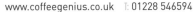

f Coffee Genius 🐦 @coffeegenius1 ✉ @coffeegenius1

№9. HOMEGROUND COFFEE + KITCHEN

Main Road, Windermere, Cumbria, LA23 1DX.

Bringing speciality coffee to the Lake District, Homeground Coffee + Kitchen showcases a rotating house espresso from Lancaster roasters J. Atkinson and Co., as well as various filter options from guest roasters such as Sundlaug, Red Bank and North Star.

Free range milk is sourced locally and can be traced to two dairy herds. You'll also find a range of leaf teas and, if you want a cheeky tipple, craft beer from the nearby Hawkshead Brewery.

INSIDER'S TIP — TRY THE DELICIOUS "SECRET RECIPE" HASH BROWNS

Food's on from 9am-3pm with imaginative brunch dishes, chunky sandwiches, huevos rancheros and the ever-popular brunch burger. There's also seasonal specials and a range of tempting cakes available.

As far as décor goes, this bustling cafe reflects the Lakes landscape with bespoke wooden furniture, slate walls and a counter created from an ash tree from owners Rich and Jane's garden.

KEY ROASTER
J. Atkinson & Co.

BREWING METHODS
Espresso, batch brew, filter, V60

MACHINE
Custom La Marzocco Linea PB 3 group

GRINDERS
Mythos One, Mahlkonig EK43

OPENING HOURS
Mon - Sun
9am-5pm
Wed Closed

Gluten FREE · COFFEE BEANS AVAILABLE · SOYA MILK AVAILABLE · CYCLE FRIENDLY · OUTDOOR SEATING · FAMILY FRIENDLY · DISABLED ACCESS

www.homegroundcafe.co.uk   T: 01539 444863

f Homeground Coffee + Kitchen   @homegroundcafe   @homegroundcafe

10. THE BRISTLY HOG COFFEE HOUSE

69 Stricklandgate, Kendal, Cumbria, LA9 4LT.

Photos: Liam Lonsdale

New on the Kendal coffee scene is The Bristly Hog, which only opened in April 2016. It's Sarah Forbes and Adam Hebbron's second coffee shop, and the one in which they've been able to create their dream speciality coffee shop with modern menu.

'Everyone comments on how cosy and welcoming it is,' says Sarah, and the friendly vibe extends to pooches as much as punters, as the couple's dog Jorgie is always on hand to hoover up dropped crumbs and meet other canine visitors.

INSIDER'S TIP: THE FAVE BREKKIE IS BRIOCHE FRENCH TOAST WITH FRESH FRUIT, HOMEMADE COULIS, MAPLE SYRUP AND CINNAMON

Local produce is a big part of the offering and the house blend coffee – as well as the decaf and single origin - come from the super local Rinaldo's. Guest coffees change all the time and are sourced from the likes of North Star in Leeds.

Complement the liquid refreshment with a menu of dishes cooked freshly to order, such as sourdough with peppery rocket, fresh mozzarella and parma ham.

KEY ROASTER
Rinaldo's Speciality Coffee & Tea

BREWING METHODS
Espresso, V60, AeroPress, batch brew

MACHINE
Kees van der Western Mirage

GRINDERS
Mahlkonig K30, Mahlkonig Vario, Anfirm Caimano, Mazzer Super Jolly

OPENING HOURS
Mon 8am-6pm
Wed-Sat 8am-6pm
Sun 10am-4pm

Gluten FREE

COFFEE BEANS AVAILABLE

SOYA MILK AVAILABLE

WIFI

CYCLE FRIENDLY

OUTDOOR seating

FAMILY FRIENDLY

DISABLED ACCESS

DOG FRIENDLY

www.thebristlyhog.com T: 01539 738785

f The Bristly Hog Coffee House @thebristlyhog @thebristlyhog

11. CARTMEL COFFEE

The Square, Cartmel, Cumbria, LA11 6QB.

Visitors flocking to the Cumbrian village of Cartmel may be seeking its rich ancient history, or booking for dinner at two Michelin-starred restaurant l'Enclume. They may even go on the trail of sticky toffee pudding – the village is said to have invented it. But whatever their reasons for venturing into Cartmel's pretty town square, they'll undoubtedly end up at Cartmel Coffee for a cracking speciality caffeine hit.

Beans come courtesy of Lancashire's J. Atkinson and Co. and the employment and training of talented baristas means the coffee is treated with care.

The coffee themed wallpaper – another indicator of Cartmel Coffee's passion for the bean – is a talking point, and whether tucked up inside, or out front at one of a couple of tables, it's a great place to sit and people watch.

INSIDER'S TIP
TRY THE AVOCADO, BACON, TOMATO AND POACHED EGG ON SOURDOUGH FOR A LUNCHTIME LIFT

The cafe is equally well known for its baked offerings, including piles of light-as-air, cream-filled meringues made with rosewater and fresh fruit, lemon meringue pie, and a good cafe menu for lunch.

KEY ROASTER
J. Atkinson & Co.

BREWING METHOD
Espresso

MACHINE
Sanremo Roma

GRINDER
Sanremo

OPENING HOURS
Mon-Sun
10am-5pm

T: 01539 535353

@cartmelcoffee

№12. THE HALL

10 China Street, Lancaster, Lancashire, LA1 1EX.

Step inside this 1936 former parish hall on Lancaster's China Street and you'll find a bakery, green bean store and of course, a cafe.

This buzzing venue is right alongside J. Atkinson and Co.'s roastery and shop and it proudly – in a relaxed, not in your face kinda way - showcases the very best of the famed roaster's current bean haul with single origins brewed on syphon and Chemex as well as served as EK43 shots.

INSIDER'S TIP VISIT FOR EVENING EVENTS AND CRAFT BEER

A coffee mecca in Lancaster, it's filled with mums, workers on their break, students and coffee connoisseurs, but don't worry, there's plenty of room. The large space has been lovingly renovated and filled with upcycled pallets and salvaged coffee machinery with a beautiful Canadian maple sprung floor (perfect for dancing) and a vaulted ceiling.

There's a great range of coffees along with the house espresso blend, Prototype, which is regularly tweaked to reflect seasonality. Also ever-changing is the range of freshly baked cakes and savouries. Visit at the weekend and you'll find evening openings, live bands and vinyl nights. Cue that dance floor ...

KEY ROASTER
J. Atkinson & Co.

BREWING METHODS
Syphon, Chemex, bulk brew, espresso

MACHINE
La Marzocco Strada

GRINDERS
Mythos, Mahlkonig EK43

OPENING HOURS
Mon-Thu
8am-6.30pm
Fri-Sat
8am-10.30pm
Sun 11am-4pm

Gluten FREE

COFFEE BEANS AVAILABLE

SOYA MILK AVAILABLE

WIFI

CYCLE FRIENDLY

COFFEE COURSES AVAILABLE

FAMILY FRIENDLY

DOG FRIENDLY

www.thecoffeehopper.com T: 01524 65470

f Priory Hall   🐦 @coffeehopper   📷 @coffeehopper

№13. THE MUSIC ROOM

Sun Square, Lancaster, Lancashire, LA1 1EW.

'*A barista's playground*' and '*laboratory of coffee gizmos*' is how roaster J. Atkinson and Co. describes its showcase cafe.

And it's well worth tracking this place down (it's tucked away in a hidden courtyard) in order to fully immerse yourself in the Atkinson coffee experience.

You'll discover its espresso blend, carefully crafted to complement the milk-based drinks and a range of black coffees, served according to the best method to highlight their complex flavours. The choice is seasonal and therefore always changing, so no visit will be the same.

INSIDER'S TIP STAY IN THE LANDMARK TRUST FLAT ABOVE THE SHOP WHICH IS DECORATED WITH THE NINE MUSES THAT INSPIRED THE SHOP'S NAME

A range of teas are given the same perfectionist treatment and a simple menu of edibles, including delicious cakes baked at sister cafe, The Hall, is also carefully selected to match the drinks.

Its relatively small, but light-filled interior has a grand baroque frontage, and if the weather allows, it's worth bagging a seat in the square to take a full gander at the impressive stonework.

KEY ROASTER
J. Atkinson & Co.

BREWING METHODS
V60, espresso, AeroPress

MACHINE
Sanremo Roma

GRINDERS
Mazzer Robur, Mythos

OPENING HOURS
Mon-Sat
10am-5pm

www.thecoffeehopper.com T: 01524 65470

f The Music Room 🐦 @coffeehopper ✉ @coffeehopper

14. EXCHANGE COFFEE COMPANY

24 Wellgate, Clitheroe, Lancashire, BB7 2DP.

This atmospheric coffee emporium is spread over three floors, with nostalgia running through all its nooks and crannies, shelves laden with coffees and related ephemera, and the aroma of freshly roasted beans everywhere.

The beans are roasted on-site in a Probat LN12 which is responsible for roasting more than 30 varieties of single origin coffees which you can buy to take home, along with a comprehensive array of equipment, from cafetieres and AeroPress to grinders.

INSIDER'S TIP
THERE ARE AT LEAST 65 DIFFERENT LOOSE LEAF TEAS AND TISANES TO TRY

If you do want to sip-in, find yourself an antique table in a William Morris wallpapered corner and imagine yourself in a Victorian coffee drinker's paradise as you order from the impressive range of Exchange coffees served as french press, drip or espresso-based drinks.

You'll also find more than 65 different loose leaf teas to sample, along with homemade soup, sandwiches, jacket potatoes and cakes.

KEY ROASTER
Exchange
Coffee Company

BREWING METHODS
Espresso,
french press,
Clever dripper

MACHINE
La Marzocco GB5

GRINDERS
Mahlkonig K30,
Mignon

OPENING HOURS
Mon-Sat
9am-5.30pm
(coffee house
closes 5pm)

 Gluten FREE

 COFFEE BEANS AVAILABLE

 SOYA MILK AVAILABLE

 WIFI

 CYCLE FRIENDLY

 OUTDOOR SEATING

 COFFEE COURSES AVAILABLE

 FAMILY FRIENDLY

---

www.exchangecoffee.co.uk   T: 01200 442270

f Exchange Coffee Company   🐦 @exchange_coffee   📷 @exchange_coffee

ATKINSONS

EST.   1837

COFFEE ROASTERS

AND

TEA MERCHANTS

ROASTED IN LANCASTER

15. EXCHANGE COFFEE COMPANY

13-15 Fleming Square, Blackburn, Lancashire, BB2 2DG.

Find your way to Fleming Square, a little street just over the road from the cathedral; sniff the air and the smell will lead you straight to one of Exchange Coffee's three retail roasting outlets.

The building itself is pretty impressive. With its stone arch frontage – complete with carved head over the door – walking in feels like an event in itself. And the first thing you'll see is the roaster, surrounded by coffee sacks. This was the original roasting shop of Exchange Coffee and the team still roasts here every day.

INSIDER'S TIP: THE GUYS HAVE A THREE-WHEELED PIAGGIO COFFEE VAN IN THE MALL, TOO

Take a wander around and marvel at the array of coffees and equipment on sale – and check out the customised Cimbali M34 espresso machine – before finding a seat in the oak panelled area downstairs, an experience which is like stepping back in time. You can also sit in the light and airy upstairs or, on a warm day, enjoy sipping coffee in the square – your alfresco dining experience enhanced by one of Exchange's cakes, or even a full Lancashire breakfast.

KEY ROASTER
Exchange Coffee Company

BREWING METHODS
Espresso, french press, Clever dripper

MACHINE
Cimbali M34

GRINDERS
Mahlkonig K30, Mignon

OPENING HOURS
Mon-Sat
9am-5.30pm (coffee house closes 5pm)

 Gluten FREE

 COFFEE BEANS AVAILABLE

 SOYA MILK AVAILABLE

 WIFI

 CYCLE FRIENDLY

 OUTDOOR SEATING

 COFFEE COURSES AVAILABLE

 FAMILY FRIENDLY

www.exchangecoffee.co.uk T: 01254 54258

f Exchange Coffee Company 🐦 @exchange_coffee 📷 @exchange_coffee

№16. HAM AND JAM COFFEE SHOP

50-52 Lancaster Road, Preston, Lancashire, PR1 1DD.

In the heart of Preston's cultural quarter, Ham and Jam not only offers unrivalled views of the Town Hall and Harris Museum from its floor to ceiling windows, but is also a welcoming community space in which to enjoy local artwork, live music and a great cup of coffee.

From writing classes to acoustic sessions, meditation evenings to art exhibitions, there's always something going on at this unique and creative cafe. The community connection continues in the coffee offering, with Lancashire roaster, J. Atkinson and Co. providing a solid seasonal blend on espresso.

INSIDER'S TIP **HAM AND JAM WAS THE CODE WORD FOR VICTORY USED BY THE BRITISH FORCES ON D DAY**

With Preston Market just a stone's throw away, the produce packing the lunch menu comes courtesy of the city's greengrocers and butchers, with artisan bread from the guys down the road at All You Knead.

The easy-going vibe here means you'll want to make time for a big old bowl of seasonal soup, a griddled panini or a slice of something sweet with your caffeine fix.

KEY ROASTER
J. Atkinsons & Co.

BREWING METHOD
Espresso

MACHINE
Sanremo Zoe

GRINDER
Sanremo

OPENING HOURS
Mon-Sat
8.30am-5.30pm
Sun 10am-4.30pm

Gluten FREE

SOYA MILK AVAILABLE

WIFI

CYCLE FRIENDLY

FAMILY Friendly

DISABLED & ACCESS

www.hamandjamcoffeeshop.com T: 01772 827430

f Ham and Jam Coffee Shop 🐦 @hamandjampr1 📷 @ham_and_jam_preston

No.17. CEDARWOOD COFFEE COMPANY

10 Winckley Street, Preston, Lancashire, PR1 2AA.

Just seconds from the city's high street, in the leafy setting of Winckley Square, Cedarwood Coffee Company is the kind of chilled out place you know you're going to enjoy.

The team clearly like to celebrate the good things in life, which is why, in addition to top notch speciality coffee you'll find oozing cakes, superb ice cream and quirky cocktails.

When it comes to the coffee, customers are spoilt for choice with espresso, french press, AeroPress and V60 methods on offer, with beans primarily coming from Lancashire's own J. Atkinson and Co. Cedarwood uses its Prototype blend – so expect a cup blooming with floral notes and soft-fruit sweetness.

INSIDER'S TIP
THE CARAMEL AFFOGATO IS A MUST – WHATEVER THE TIME OF YEAR

Take your caffeine hit at the ground level espresso bar, then follow it, later in the day, with something a little stronger at the upstairs bar, where you'll discover a selection of craft ales, beers and ciders.

KEY ROASTER
J. Atkinson & Co.

BREWING METHODS
Espresso, V60, AeroPress, french press

MACHINE
Sanremo Verona

GRINDER
Sanremo

OPENING HOURS
Mon-Fri 8am-5pm
Sat-Sun 11am-5pm

 COFFEE BEANS AVAILABLE

 SOYA MILK AVAILABLE

 WIFI

  OUTDOOR SEATING

---

www.cedarwood.coffee   T: 01772 821769

f Cedarwood Coffee Co.   @winckleystreet   @cedarwoodcoffeeco

18. CAFFÈ & CO.

8 Dane Court, Rainhill, Prescot, Merseyside, L35 4LU.

If you have an epiphany and realise that crafting coffee is your real calling while sipping a silky flat white at Caffè & Co. in Rainhill, you're in the right place as this neighbourhood cafe doubles up as a barista training school.

Serving speciality coffee by day and coaching the next generation of baristas by night, owner Neil Osthoff has transformed the former village bank into a coffee emporium.

Locals flock here for a quality caffeine fix, with a good range of guest single origins and a well-equipped brew bar promising a compelling cup, with budding baristas making the journey for SCAE-trained Neil's courses, covering everything from basic espresso skills to the complete speciality shop set-up.

INSIDER'S TIP GRAB A SEAT ON THE GRASSY SEATING AREA IF THE SUN'S ON YOUR SIDE

More than 20 flavours of ice cream, traditional crêpes and fruit-packed smoothies make Caffè & Co. a must for coffee lovers of the sweet-toothed variety, while there are hearty Irish breakfasts and chunky sarnies for those after something a little more substantial.

KEY ROASTER
Allpress

BREWING METHODS
Espresso, V60, AeroPress, french press, Chemex

MACHINE
La Marzocco GB5 3 Group

GRINDER
Mythos One

OPENING HOURS
Mon-Fri
8.30am-4.30pm
Sat 9am-4.30pm
Sun 10.30am-2.30pm

SOYA MILK AVAILABLE

WIFI

CYCLE FRIENDLY

OUTDOOR SEATING

COFFEE COURSES AVAILABLE

FAMILY FRIENDLY

DISABLED ACCESS

www.caffeandco.com T: 01514 932332

f Caffè & Co.   @caffeandco

№ 19. PANNA

Silkhouse Court, Tithebarn Street, Liverpool, Merseyside, L2 2LZ.

Just around the corner from a large Costa in the bustling commercial quarter of the city, Panna is converting the worker bees to speciality coffee – including the staff from the aforementioned chain, who now go to Panna for their coffee break. Funny that.

Brewing up beans from Liverpool's own Neighbourhood Coffee, as well as Has Bean and Workshop, Peter and Ivana are showcasing what carefully sourced and roasted coffee tastes like, and introducing people to the pleasures of the pourover and AeroPress, as well as espresso-based coffee.

INSIDER'S TIP
LOOK OUT FOR THE LAUNCH OF THE EVENING FOOD AND COFFEE EVENTS

Three years old, Panna is one of the originals in the city, probably only second to Bold Street Cafe in flying the flag for speciality coffee. The Slovakian couple have brought their own unique twist to the genre, introducing the concepts of Scandinavian fika, kavicka and descanso para el cafe to the city, alongside a smörgåsbord of European inspired freshly-made soups, sarnies and artisan French baguettes. If you're lunching, go early as it gets rammed – at other times, it's a quiet sanctuary from the frenetic city outside.

KEY ROASTER
Has Bean

BREWING METHODS
Espresso,
V60, AeroPress,
Chemex,
cold brew

MACHINE
La Spaziale S5

GRINDER
La Spaziale 12
grind on demand

OPENING HOURS
Mon-Fri
8am-4.30pm

Gluten FREE

COFFEE BEANS AVAILABLE

SOYA MILK AVAILABLE

WIFI

CYCLE FRIENDLY

OUTDOOR seating

FAMILY FRIENDLY

www.pannaliverpool.com   T: 01512 274764

f PANNA   @pannaliverpool

№20. ROOT COFFEE

50-52 Hanover Street, Liverpool, Merseyside, L1 4AF.

The newcomer to Liverpool's burgeoning speciality coffee scene, Root only opened its doors at the end of 2015.

The team's ethos in creating this large, airy joint is about the simple joy of making something good, and they're ticking all the boxes: serving quality speciality roasts with precision (weighing every dose), and adding a little theatre with the pourover section on the brew bar. Then there are the high quality teas and cascara, and nice touches such as furniture and cladding upcycled from abandoned pallets reclaimed from the docks.

INSIDER'S TIP SIGN UP FOR AN AFTER-HOURS HOME BREWING SESSION, WHERE THE GUYS PROVIDE ADVICE ON HOW TO GET THE BEST OUT OF YOUR EQUIPMENT

With lots of outdoor seating just off busy Hanover Street, summer should see Root come into its own, but whatever the weather, it's a serene spot to work, meet friends and enjoy good coffee.

With a plan to be constantly progressive and help push the speciality coffee market forward in Liverpool, we think this is one that's going to take root.

KEY ROASTERS
Extract Coffee Roasters,
Round Hill Roastery

BREWING METHODS
Espresso, V60,
AeroPress

MACHINE
Victoria Arduino
VA388
Gravimetric
Black Eagle

GRINDERS
Mythos One,
Mahlkonig EK43

OPENING HOURS
Mon-Sat 8am-7pm
Sun 9am-6pm

Gluten FREE

COFFEE BEANS AVAILABLE

SOYA MILK AVAILABLE

WIFI

CYCLE FRIENDLY

OUTDOOR SEATING

FAMILY FRIENDLY

DISABLED ACCESS

---

www.rootcoffee.co.uk

Root Coffee   @rootcoffeeliv   @rootcoffeeliv

21. BOLD STREET COFFEE

89 Bold Street, Liverpool, Merseyside, L1 4HF.

The originators of the speciality scene in Liverpool, Bold Street Coffee began life as a team of nomadic baristas serving coffee to festival goers in fields across the UK. And for quite some time, after the Bold Street location was launched in 2010, it was the only place to find carefully sourced, speciality grade coffee in the city.

INSIDER'S TIP **LOOK OUT FOR OCCASIONAL MUSIC EVENTS**

Things have moved on as additional coffee shops have popped up, but Bold Street still takes some beating for the quality of its brews, breakfasts and music via vinyl on a couple of Technics behind the bar.

The team experiment with a number of roasters along with its house beans from Has Bean, which goes down well with the legion of laptop warriors who get their daily caffeine fix at the cafe.

Breakfast is really good, and the french toast with bacon and maple syrup, porridge with a range of fruity and nutty accompaniments, and the bacon butties all worth making a bee-line for. And with a friendly vibe, a selection of coffee serve styles, guest roasts, brewing gear for sale and simple, contemporary decor, it's a must-visit.

KEY ROASTERS
Has Bean,
Square Mile,
Workshop,
The Barn

BREWING METHODS
Espresso,
AeroPress,
Chemex

MACHINE
La Marzocco
Linea PB

GRINDERS
Mazzer Robur E,
Mahlkonig EK43,
Mythos

OPENING HOURS
Mon-Fri
7.30am-6pm
Sat 8am-6pm
Sun 9am-5pm

www.boldstreetcoffee.co.uk

Bold Street Coffee   @boldstcoffee   @boldstreetcoffee

№22. 92 DEGREES COFFEE

24 Hardman Street, Liverpool, Merseyside, L1 9AX.

The first combined cafe and micro-roastery in Liverpool, 92 Degrees serves coffee that's roasted in-house in small batches, so freshness is guaranteed.

As a result of its unusual dual role, the team prides itself on knowing about the farmer who produced the coffee and sharing that information with customers who want to dig a little deeper.

'We aim to get across the fact that the price a customer pays for their coffee is worth it because they are supporting people who are farming in some of the poorest parts of the world,' says owner Danny Marfany.

INSIDER'S TIP CHECK OUT DANNY'S NEW DIGS, REX, NEXT TO THE CITY'S CENTRAL STATION

However, there are lots of other, purely selfish, reasons to visit this beautifully light cafe, housed in the city's first police station. Doorstop sarnies, generous bagels and ciabatta all stuffed with locally sourced fillings are supported by a fine cast of cakes (including enormous homemade Jaffa Cakes) and loose leaf teas. Grab a stool at the long bar and enjoy watching the world going by from the huge windows, as you take a coffee adventure to the far reaches of the globe.

KEY ROASTER
92 Degrees Coffee

BREWING METHODS
Espresso, V60

MACHINES
Wega Concept Duo,
Expobar Diamant 3

GRINDER
Mazzer Super Jolly

OPENING HOURS
Mon-Fri
7.45am-7pm
Sat 10am-7pm
Sun 10am-6pm

GLUTEN FREE

COFFEE BEANS AVAILABLE

SOYA MILK AVAILABLE

WIFI

CYCLE FRIENDLY

OUTDOOR SEATING

FAMILY FRIENDLY

DISABLED ACCESS

DOG FRIENDLY

www.92degreescoffee.com   T: 01517 091145

f 92DegreesCoffee   🐦 @92degreescoffee   ✉ @92degreescoffee

№23. JUNCTION COFFEE

305 Aigburth Road, Liverpool, Merseyside, L17 0BJ.

It's the sign of speciality coffee coming of age in a city when it's available to the wider population, not just a hardcore group of hipsters.

So it's fantastic to discover Junction Coffee at a shopping precinct on the busy Aigburth Road, populated by mums and kids after school, nannas from the nearby old folks' home and electricians pulling in for elevenses.

'Why shouldn't we serve great coffee, just because we're not in the city centre?' questions owner, Nathan Chesney. *'We do get coffee geeks tracking us down, and I love that, but I also enjoy being part of the community.'*

Serving a range of single origins as Kalita Wave (*'for a clean cup'*) and a house blend made by Has Bean, Junction is on a mission to educate people about good coffee. *'We encourage people to try our great coffees from all over the world,'* says Nathan, but he recognises that as a community cafe, it's important to provide quality coffee in every cup, regardless of preference.

KEY ROASTER
Has Bean

BREWING METHODS
Espresso,
Kalita Wave

MACHINE
La Spaziale S5

GRINDER
Mahlkonig Vario
K30

OPENING HOURS
Mon-Fri
8am-5.15pm
Sat 9.30am-5.15pm

INSIDER'S TIP A LOCAL CHAP MAKES CAKES JUST FOR JUNCTION - INCLUDING GLUTEN-FREE GOODIES

www.junctioncoffee.co.uk T: 01517 271070

f Junction Coffee   @junctioncoffee

Drinks
Gear
Knowledge

The home of Sweetbird, Zuma and Cosy Tea has been supplying the coffee scene for over 18 years, and is a proud supporter of the Northern Coffee Guide

0117 953 3522
ⓦⓨⓕ @beyondthebean

№24. PROVIDERO

148 Conwy Road, Llandudno Junction, Conwy, LL31 9DU.

After a few years making coffee along the coast of north Wales from the back of a 40-year-old Citroen van, Jon Hughes felt it was time for a more permanent base.

A successful crowdsourcing campaign later, in 2014 he was able to open the doors of a new venture, the Providero Coffee shop at Llandudno Junction.

As if he needed any further evidence of its popularity (more than 150 coffee fans pledged support for the Kickstarter project), Providero has gone on to attract such legions of fans that there are plans to open another cafe in Llandudno later this year.

His secret? *'We try to do just a few things, but do them well,'* says Jon. *'We have three espresso-based coffees on daily: our house blend, a decaf option and a single origin of the month, while we also serve single origin coffee as bulk brew, AeroPress and Clever dripper.'*

On top of that, there are around 30 varieties of loose leaf tea, coffee paraphernalia to buy and extras like hot choc sticks handmade by a local chocolatier. All the cakes are homemade, including vegan and gluten-free options, and you can also indulge in artisan bread, toast and jams from nearby micro-bakeries.

KEY ROASTER
Heartland Coffi

BREWING METHODS
Espresso, filter (bulk brew), AeroPress, Clever dripper, Cona

MACHINE
La Marzocco Linea 2 group

GRINDERS
Mythos One, Mahlkonig Vario

OPENING HOURS
Mon-Fri 8am-6pm
Sat 9am-6pm

INSIDER'S TIP WE LIKE THE BYO LUNCH POLICY

www.providero.co.uk

Providero: Fine Teas & Coffees @providero @providerolife

& CO. | J. ATKINSON & CO. | J. ATKINSON & CO.
LOOSE LEAF | ESSPRESSO
TEAS — | BLEND —

6,50 | 7,50

— †12,50 EACH (LOCALLY MADE

WHAT'S THAT

- Macchiato:
  — STEAMED MILK
  — 2 SHOTS ESPRES
- SERVED IN ESPRESSO CUP 2 O
- Cortado:
  — STEAMED MILK
  — 2 SHOTS ESPRESSO
- SERVED IN A SMALL GLASS L
- FLAT WHITE:
  — STEAMED MILK
  — 2 SHOTS ESPRESSO
- SERVED IN TULIP CUP 6oz

AMERICANO:

2 SHOTS
ESPRESSO +
HOT WATER —
MILK SERVED
ON THE SIDE
- SERVED IN A 12oz CUP

FILTER:

BULK BREW
PROCESS, BEANS
FROM ONE SINGLE
ORAGIN
- SERVED IN A 12oz CUP

"WE SERVE ARCHETYPE ESPRE
BLEND, ROASTED BY J. ATKINSON
& CO. LANCASTER."

FRES
FRUI
70

CAKE
POPS

GREATER
MANCHESTER
& CHESHIRE

№25. ANCOATS COFFEE CO.

Unit 9, Royal Mills, 17 Redhill Street, Ancoats, Manchester, M4 5BA.

From the heart of the industrial revolution to the heart of the northern coffee revolution, Ancoats is turning cotton into silk.

When last year's *Indy Coffee Guide* went to press, Jamie Boland was roasting out of a chilly industrial unit in the Ancoats part of the city, with plans to create a cafe/roastery nearby. So it's stunning to see what he's created just one year on.

Converting part of a historic former cotton mill into a cafe with roastery on site, the vibe is high spec, industrial and yet cosy, with vaulted brick ceilings and tables formed around imposing steel columns.

With the roaster positioned in the middle, there's an unbeatable bit of theatre going on as you sip your Warehouse City seasonal espresso blend (or one of the other rotating single blend espresso or pourover coffees) and dig into the simple, seasonal cafe menu.

KEY ROASTER
Ancoats Coffee Co.

BREWING METHODS
Espresso, V60, AeroPress, Chemex, Pheonix 70, cold brew

MACHINE
Nuevo Simonelli Aurelia II Digi

GRINDER
Mythos One

OPENING HOURS
Mon-Fri 7am-5pm
Sat-Sun 9am-5pm

INSIDER'S TIP CHECK OUT THE MONTHLY SUPPER CLUB WHERE LOCAL CHEFS TAKE OVER THE SPACE FOR THE EVENING

www.ancoats-coffee.co.uk T: 01612 283211

f Ancoats Coffee Co. 🐦 @ancoatscoffee 📷 @ancoatscoffeeco

№26. TAKK COFFEE HOUSE

6 Tariff Street, Manchester, M1 2FF.

Nordic meets Manchester at Tariff Street's coffee HQ. Don't be shy to shimmy up to the brew bar and ask the baristas for what's good, because Takk showcases interesting coffees and roasters from across the world.

The team has just released the fifth incarnation of its Nordic-style house espresso which is a single origin sourced directly for Takk by Clifton Coffee Roasters. The Finka Miravalle comes from a Cup of Excellence farm in El Salvador, and Takk owner Philip Hannaway describes it as, *'hitting the spot between sweetness and acidity'.*

INSIDER'S TIP LOOK OUT FOR FREE OPEN-CUPPING SESSIONS THROUGHOUT THE YEAR AND COLD BREW MASTERCLASSES IN SUMMER

In addition, the team's also introduced milk from a single herd, via Stephensons Dairy in Morecambe, and beefed up the weekend brunch menu to include dishes such as steak and eggs, Mexican-style. The food's really good BTW, and more than just an adjunct to the coffee. The result of all these developments is that business is booming, with exciting plans for expansion over the next few years.

KEY ROASTER
Clifton Coffee Roasters

BREWING METHODS
Espresso, Chemex, AeroPress, Toddy, tower cold brew

MACHINE
La Marzocco Linea PB

GRINDERS
Mahlkonig K30, Mahlkonig EK43, Mythos

OPENING HOURS
Mon-Fri
8am-5pm
Sat 9am-5pm
Sun 10am-5pm

www.takkmcr.com

Takk @takkmcr @takkmcr

Nº27. FIG + SPARROW

20 Oldham Street, Manchester, M1 1JN.

The pursuit of beauty (along with a shot of coffee) is clearly what gets Fig + Sparrow owners Jan and Emily Dixon up in the morning.

Their Northern Quarter coffee shop, lifestyle and gift store is stuffed to the rafters with design-led artefacts and ephemera, from jewel-like porcelain bowls to the gleaming copper coloured V60s on the brew bar.

It's a creative and inspiring spot to stop by for a coffee, and the quality applies to the drinks too, with Climpson & Sons Estate Blend used in the espresso menu, along with a guest seasonal coffee called The Fields, and regularly rotating single origins.

INSIDER'S TIP: DISCOVER SEVEN ALTERNATIVE MILKS AND BARISTAS WHO KNOW HOW TO USE IT

Alluringly decorated cakes continue the aesthetic theme, along with a comforting cafe menu, while the cafe's Airbnb apartment nearby allows guests to live the Fig + Sparrow lifestyle on visits to the city.

KEY ROASTER
Climpson & Sons

BREWING METHODS
Espresso, V60, AeroPress, Chemex

MACHINE
La Marzocco Linea PB AV2

GRINDERS
Mahlkonig EK43, Mazzer Major Electronic

OPENING HOURS
Mon-Fri 8am-7pm
Sat 10am-6pm
Sun 11am-6pm

www.figandsparrow.co.uk T: 01612 281843

f Fig + Sparrow 🐦 @figsparrow 📷 @figsparrow

MCR 28. TEACUP KITCHEN

55 Thomas Street, Northern Quarter, Manchester, M4 1NA.

Who could fail to fall in love with Teacup Kitchen for its stack of foot-high cakes, massive selection of loose leaf teas, delicious rustic and hearty food and, of course, speciality coffee?

No-one with any sense is the answer, which is why it's been a foodie favourite in the creative Northern Quarter for almost a decade, holds the title for Most Innovative Breakfast and has been included in *The Good Food Guide* for three years.

INSIDER'S TIP CHECK OUT SISTER VENUES PROPER TEA, BONBON, THE CAFE AT THE MUSEUM AND TEACUP CAKERY

The breakfast award refers to its Exoticado Eggs, a combination of a poached duck egg, pan fried exotic mushrooms and avocado on toast, which is consistently on the menu – and best accompanied by a flat white and the Sunday papers.

The house espresso blend comes from Brazil, Honduras and El Salvador by way of Butterworth and Son in Bury St Edmunds, and there's a single origin from Colombia available (through the french press and as a V60), too.

KEY ROASTER
Butterworth and Son

BREWING METHODS
French press, V60, espresso

MACHINE
La Marzocco

GRINDER
Anfim Milano

OPENING HOURS
Sun-Mon
10am-6pm
Tue-Sat
10am-late

www.teacupandcakes.com   T: 01618 323233

f Teacup Kitchen   @teacupandcakes   @teacupandcakes

29. FEDERAL CAFE & BAR

9 Nicholas Croft, Manchester, M4 1EY.

Bringing a blast of sunny Antipodean cafe culture to Manchester's Northern Quarter, Federal is a funky new find for great coffee and rustic, homemade tucker, in equal measure.

With halloumi and 'shrooms on sourdough, eggs done any way, Emily's banana bread, french toast with berries, whipped mascarpone and salted caramel, along with corn fritter stacks with bacon, fried eggs, tomatoes, Sriracha and rocket ... well, you could stay here all day.

INSIDER'S TIP TAKE A TRIP DOWN UNDER WITH VEGEMITE ON TOAST, ANZAC BICKIES, PINEAPPLE LAMINGTONS AND FLOWERS IN BUNDABERG BOTTLES

So squeeze up on one of the little tables (it gets wildly busy, especially at weekend brunch-time), and enjoy the quirky décor and a buzz that comes from more than just the Ozone-roasted house blend in your flat white.

Single origins provide even more delight, served as filter, V60 and AeroPress, with cold brew on hand for sunny days. It's bonzer.

KEY ROASTER
Ozone Coffee
Roasters

BREWING METHODS
Espresso, V60,
AeroPress,
cold brew, filter

MACHINE
La Marzocco
Linea PB

GRINDERS
Mazzer Robur,
Mahlkonig EK43

OPENING HOURS
Mon-Fri
7.30am-8pm
Sat 9am-8pm
Sun 9am-5pm

Gluten FREE

COFFEE BEANS AVAILABLE

SOYA MILK AVAILABLE

WIFI

CYCLE FRIENDLY

OUTDOOR seating

DOG FRIENDLY

www.federalcafe.co.uk   T: 01614 250974

f Federal Cafe & Bar   @federalcafebar   @federalcafebar

NR. 30. GRINDSMITH POD

Greengate Square, Victoria Bridge Street, Manchester, M3 5AS.

The Pod on Greengate Square is where it all started for the Grindsmith crew. Created as a result of a crowdfunding campaign in 2014, it's the metaphorical home of the mini coffee empire which now has three outposts across Manchester.

A sun trap in summer, it's a good cycle pit spot in the city where you can park your two wheels and fuel up on locally roasted coffee.

Take it as a simple flat white, or explore a whole raft of contemporary serve styles – from Chemex to AeroPress. It's Fido-friendly too, naturally.

INSIDER'S TIP THE COFFEE'S NOT THE ONLY THING THAT'S GOLD STAR ABOUT GRINDSMITH – WE LIKE ITS GOLD TEASPOONS TOO

As in its big brother establishments, you'll find a range of guest roasters such as Drop Coffee on the menu, along with the locally-roasted, house Heart and Graft beans: *'It's where we get our coffee geek on,'* says owner Charlie Hooson-Sykes.

KEY ROASTER
Heart and Graft

BREWING METHODS
Espresso, filter, Kalita, Chemex, syphon, AeroPress

MACHINE
La Marzocco GS3

GRINDER
Mythos

OPENING HOURS
Mon-Sat 8am-5pm
Sun 9am-5pm

 Gluten FREE

 COFFEE BEANS AVAILABLE

 SOYA MILK AVAILABLE

 WIFI

 CYCLE FRIENDLY

 OUTDOOR SEATING

 DOG FRIENDLY

www.grindsmith.com T: 07740 357436

f Grindsmith @grindsmiths @grindsmiths

31. POT KETTLE BLACK

Barton Arcade, Deansgate, Manchester, M3 2BW.

Just because you're shopping in the middle of Manchester's busy Deansgate and St Anne's Square, with their big brand stores, it doesn't mean that coffee at a Costa is the only option.

Because if you step inside the Victorian Barton Arcade - which sits between the two hotspots - you'll discover an indie coffee shop that's a haven of hospitality and an escape from the bustle.

INSIDER'S TIP PULL UP A STOOL AT THE CENTRAL TABLE AND GET STUCK INTO SOME WORK OR A GOOD BOOK WITH YOUR FELLOW COFFEE FIENDS

This elegant yet contemporary cafe was set up by a couple of professional rugby players who were inspired by the vibrant Sydney coffee scene that they'd experienced on their travels. And PKB does good service to its Aussie inspiration, employing talented baristas to brew up speciality coffee from the likes of Workshop and Origin.

Choose espresso-based drinks or go cold-drip, V60 or AeroPress. It's all good, as they say Down Under.

KEY ROASTER
Workshop

BREWING METHODS
Espresso,
AeroPress, V60,
cold drip

MACHINE
La Marzocco
Linea PB

GRINDER
Mythos

OPENING HOURS
Mon-Fri 8am-7pm
Sat 9am-7pm
Sun 10am-5pm

www.potkettleblackltd.co.uk

Pot Kettle Black Ltd @pkbcoffee @pkbcoffee

32. GRINDSMITH ESPRESSO & BREWBAR

231-233 Deansgate, Manchester, M3 4EN.

Since last year's guide, Grindsmith's taken the lower end of Deansgate by storm, luring coffee geeks out of the Northern Quarter as it's developed its hot desk/workspace (AKA Manchester Rise) cafe concept.

Ten new permanent office spaces upstairs, along with lots more hot desks has seen the team go from serving 50 cups of coffee a day to 250. Not that the quality has suffered, as owners Pete, Luke and team are 100 per cent focused on quality of brew, a good menu in the licenced cafe, and upbeat service.

INSIDER'S TIP REGULAR EVENTS AT THE DEANSGATE SITE INCLUDE FORTNIGHTLY MANIFESTO LIVE MUSIC NIGHTS

Using beans from the city's Heart and Graft Coffee Roastery, alongside a number of guest roasters, they serve coffee as single origin espresso, syphon, Chemex, pourover and cold brew. No doubt the latter will be popular in summertime, if the team finally gets its long-awaited permission for pavement seating.

KEY ROASTER
Heart and Graft

BREWING METHODS
Espresso, syphon, Kalita, Chemex, AeroPress, filter, cold brew

MACHINE
Black Eagle 2 group

GRINDERS
Mythos, Mahlkonig EK43

OPENING HOURS
Mon-Sat 8am-8pm
Sun 9am-5pm

 Gluten FREE

 COFFEE BEANS AVAILABLE

 SOYA MILK AVAILABLE

 WIFI

 DOG FRIENDLY

www.grindsmith.com T: 01614 084699

f Grindsmith 🐦 @grindsmith_gn ✉ @grindsmiths

№33. GRINDSMITH MEDIA CITY

Media City, Salford, Greater Manchester, M50 2TG.

A n exciting development for both the team behind Grindsmith and the workers at Manchester's Media City, is the opening of Grindsmith's new gaff in Salford.

The impressive site is spread over two floors and serves great speciality coffee along with cocktails, wine and beer. There's also a small but perfectly formed menu covering breakfast, brunch, lunch and dinner. And it's all interspersed with quality teas and cakes throughout the day.

INSIDER'S TIP CHECK OUT THE SPECIALITY TEAS SERVED IN A SYPHON – VERY NOW

International roasters such as Stockholm's Drop Coffee sit alongside Manchester's own Heart and Graft, with others such as J. Atkinson and Co. and Leeds' North Star besides.

For those working at Media City, it's a must-visit for that first coffee of the day, through to after dinner drinks and cocktails courtesy of world renowned bartender the 'Cocktail Hobbit'. Lucky them.

KEY ROASTER
Heart and Graft

BREWING METHODS
Espresso, filter, Kalita, Chemex, syphon, AeroPress

MACHINE
Black Eagle 3 group

GRINDERS
Mythos, Mahlkonig EK43

OPENING HOURS
Mon-Sat
7.30am-8pm
Sun 9am-5pm

www.grindsmith.com T: 07740 357436

 Grindsmith @grindsmith_mc @grindsmiths

№34. CAFFEINE AND CO

Longford Park, Manchester, M32 8DA.

If the smell of ground coffee doesn't draw you into Caffeine and Co in Manchester's Longford Park, the waft of freshly baked bread from the in-house bakery should do the trick.

Already boasting the best spot in the park – opposite the swings and next to pet's corner, duh – the super family-friendly cafe is also luring in locals with arguably the best foodie combo (sorry fish and chips): coffee and cake.

INSIDER'S TIP GET HERE EARLY FOR BACON SARNIES WITH BREAD STILL WARM FROM THE OVEN

On the caffeine front, rich and sweet espresso-style milk drinks and clean filter brews are the house faves, made from a line-up of mainly single origins from Dark Woods, Five Elephant and Origin, among others.

And when it comes to the accompanying treat, a marriage of traditional baking techniques and fresh inspiration ensures an intriguing range of luscious loaf cakes and top-notch tray bakes for the perfect pairing.

The bakery's cranking out beautiful sourdough, quiches and pies too, so grab a seat outside for an alfresco lunch if you can.

KEY ROASTERS
Origin,
Heart and Graft

BREWING METHODS
Espresso, drip

MACHINE
Nuova Simonelli T3

GRINDERS
Mythos One,
Mahlkonig EK43

OPENING HOURS
Mon-Fri 10am-5pm
Sat 9.30am-5pm
Sun 10am-5pm

 Gluten FREE

 COFFEE BEANS AVAILABLE

 SOYA MILK AVAILABLE

 CYCLE FRIENDLY

 OUTDOOR seating

 FAMILY friendly

 DISABLED ACCESS

DOG FRIENDLY

www.caffeineandco.com   T:07778 784440

f Caffeine & Co   🐦 @caffeineandco

№35. COFFEE FIX

80 Church Road, Gatley, Stockport, Greater Manchester, SK8 4NQ.

You'll find all walks of life at Coffee Fix in Gatley, from weary walkers with muddy pawed friends in tow to the town's new breed of coffee connoisseurs, and that's just how brother and sister team Gareth and Claira like it.

Bringing speciality brew to the suburbs of Stockport, what started out as a rather risky investment in a coffee van has matured into a thriving community cafe. Manchester's Heart and Graft is the staple in the grinders, with guest roasts from around the country featuring on the brew bar, so everyone is catered for, from the regulars who know how they like it, to those up for something new.

INSIDER'S TIP GRAB YOUR LYCRA, COFFEE FIX IS A POPULAR HANGOUT WITH CYCLISTS

Just as with the coffee, great care and attention is paid to the sourcing of produce for the other menus, so you'll find artisan producers stocking the bar with craft beer, and local ingredients in the lunch offerings and indulgent cakes.

KEY ROASTER
Heart and Graft

BREWING METHODS
Espresso,
AeroPress,
pourover

MACHINE
Astoria

GRINDERS
Anfim, Mazzer

OPENING HOURS
Mon-Fri
9am-4.30pm
Sun 10am-4.30pm

www.wearecoffeefix.com T: 01612 820090

f Coffee Fix 🐦 @coffee_fix 📷 @wearecoffeefix

№36. MARKET HOUSE COFFEE

Market House, Market Street, Altrincham, Cheshire, WA14 1SA.

Photos: Claire Harrison@Momentspictured

At the heart of a restored and award winning market (named Best Market in the *Observer Food Monthly* Awards 2015), a trip to this coffee outlet is a real event, and as much about a celebration of community and local spirit, as it is about coffee.

Not only do you get to indulge in a perfect cup of Atkinson's fresh roast, Archetype, or one of the rotating single origin blends, but you also get to soak up the surrounding atmosphere.

INSIDER'S TIP
TROVE BAKERY SOURDOUGH TOAST AND MARMALADE WITH ATKINSON COFFEE - WHAT A WAY TO START THE DAY ...

Altrincham Market was closed, restored to its original shop front layout and reopened in 2014, much to the delight of the locals, who consequently saw a return of high quality and local foods to their town.

So grab a coffee and freshly made cantuccini, biscotti or granola bar, and sit at one of communal wooden tables and take in all the action. You can also try out the market's other foodie offerings, including steaks and pizza, pies, cakes, wines and craft beers. Oh, and the vin santo and amaretti is pretty special, too.

KEY ROASTER
J. Atkinson & Co.

BREWING METHODS
Espresso, filter

MACHINE
Sanremo Verona 3 group

GRINDER
Sanremo SR70

OPENING HOURS
Tue-Sat
9am-10pm
Sun 9am-6pm

 Gluten FREE

 COFFEE BEANS AVAILABLE

 SOYA MILK AVAILABLE

 WIFI

 CYCLE FRIENDLY

 OUTDOOR SEATING

 FAMILY FRIENDLY

 DISABLED ACCESS

 DOG FRIENDLY

www.altrinchammarket.co.uk T: 01619 414261
f Altrincham Market @mkthousecoffee @altymarket

e:		loose leaf tea:	
so	2.20	english breakfast	2.30
ack	2.40	pure himalayan darjeeling	2.50
ccino	2.60	china green sencha	2.40
	2.60	jasmine green	2.30
ano	2.40	classic earl grey	2.30
	2.70	samovar orange spice	2.60
hite	2.60	mint marrakech	2.60
iato	2.30	organic peppermint	2.30
sino	2.30	organic pure rooibos	2.30
lo or piccolo	2.50	organic pure camomile	2.30
ocolate	2.60		

ard we make our coffees with whole milk, just ask if you would prefer semi, skimmed or soya

r milk comes straight from a local dairy

NORTH & WEST YORKSHIRE

No. **37.** YAY COFFEE!

12a York Place, Scarborough, North Yorkshire, YO11 2NP.

Tucked away in a basement just off Scarborough's High Street, Yay Coffee is a little craft coffee shop that's quickly becoming a speciality hotspot in the town.

It's run by Rob and Lottie who say, *'our mission is simple: to make great coffee that's accessible to everyone – and to have fun doing it'.*

Yay's main focus is on single origin filter coffee and espresso, and it regularly rotates the beans on offer, while Bristol's excellent Extract Coffee Roasters remains the house choice. There's something for everyone on offer here though, with quality the thread that runs throughout, so it also serves award-winning Kokoa Collection hot chocolate and Canton Tea.

INSIDER'S TIP
GRAB A SUMMERTIME E&T – ESPRESSO PULLED OVER ICED MEDITERRANEAN TONIC WATER

In summer, look out for the newly stocked cold brew cartons for a chilled blast, and supplement all that caffeine with breakfast, fresh, well-filled bagels and sweet treats.

KEY ROASTER
Extract Coffee Roasters

BREWING METHODS
Espresso, filter, cold brew

MACHINE
Sanremo Verona RS

GRINDERS
K30 twin, Vario

OPENING HOURS
Mon-Fri 8am-6pm
Sat 9am-5pm

 Gluten FREE

 COFFEE BEANS AVAILABLE

 SOYA MILK AVAILABLE

 WIFI

 CYCLE FRIENDLY

 COFFEE COURSES AVAILABLE

www.yaycoffee.com   T: 01723 364133

f Yay Coffee Scarborough   ⊎ @yaycoffeeuk   ⊠ @yaycoffeeuk

№38. BREW & BROWNIE

5 Museum Street, York, North Yorkshire, YO1 7DT.

Good luck scoring a table at this bustling coffee spot just over the road from York's Museum Gardens, as Brew & Brownie has got a loyal following of both locals and tourists addicted to its bakes.

Sticking around for a seat is well worth the wait however, because if the rustic counter stacked high with freshly made tray bakes and sweet pastries doesn't see you cutting ties with your self-restraint, it'll be the cracking coffee that accompanies them.

INSIDER'S TIP
TRY AND RESIST THE PANCAKES PILED HIGH WITH BACON, BLUEBERRIES AND SYRUP, WE DARE YOU

Award winning beans from Carvetii Coffee in Cumbria are the go-to choice for espresso, while there's also a selection of other speciality roasters such as Dark Woods and Workshop available to sample on the AeroPress.

Local artisan food producers get a look in on the extensive breakfast and brunching options here too: doorstop bacon sarnie with bread from local bakers, the Wilson's of York pork pie, and the smashed avo on sourdough with poached eggs.

KEY ROASTER
Carvetii Coffee

BREWING METHODS
Espresso,
AeroPress

MACHINE
Sanremo Verona

GRINDER
Mahlkonig K30

OPENING HOURS
Mon-Sat 9am-5pm
Sun 10am-4pm

Gluten FREE

COFFEE BEANS AVAILABLE

SOYA MILK AVAILABLE

---

www.brewandbrownie.com   T: 01904 647420

f Brew & Brownie   🐦 @brewandbrownie   📷 @brewandbrownie

№39. THE ATTIC AND CAFE HARLEQUIN

2 King's Square, York, North Yorkshire, YO1 8BH.

With nine brew methods and 15 Has Bean single origins to choose from, it's a pretty safe bet that even the most seasoned coffee connoisseur will find something novel at The Attic and Cafe Harlequin in York. And with 2015 UK Brewers Cup champion, Gordon Howell, at the helm, you're in for a winning cup whatever you plump for.

Split over two levels in a beautiful old building in the city's historic centre, head to the first floor cafe for traditional cream teas, savoury snacks and homemade treats, or The Attic (another floor up), for an eclectic mix of local artwork and a cracking craft beer line-up which comes to life after dark on Thursday, Friday and Saturday evenings.

INSIDER'S TIP SAMPLE MORE THAN 70 TYPES OF GIN AT THE ATTIC

Although you can sip speciality coffee at the cafe, the latter is where the caffeine sorcery gets really geeky. And in addition to keeping five grinders on the go and pulling shots through the two customised machines, Gordon also regularly holds SCAE brewing and barista masterclasses.

KEY ROASTER
Has Bean

BREWING METHODS
Espresso, EK shots, Kalita, V60, Clever dripper, Chemex, french press, filter, AeroPress

MACHINES
Nuova Simonelli Competizione WBC 2010, Dalla Corte Evolution

GRINDERS
Clima Pro, K30, Ditting 1203, Anfim Barista, Mahlkonig EK43

OPENING HOURS
Cafe Harlequin:
Mon-Fri 10am-4pm
Sat 10am-5pm
Sun 10.30am-3.30pm

The Attic:
Thu-Sat
12pm-11pm

www.harlequinyork.com T: 01904 630631
f The attic (at harlequins) 🐦 @harlequinyork

40. THE FOSSGATE SOCIAL

25 Fossgate, York, North Yorkshire, YO10 5AY.

Proud of its place in York's thriving independent foodie quarter, The Fossgate Social is the kind of cafe you wish was your local.

Social is the watchword here and friendly staff and a don't-worry-about-a-thing atmosphere means you can make yourself comfy at this family-run coffee spot.

So pack a book, sink into a sofa and take time over the house North Star espresso blend and a sizzling artisan sandwich, hot off the griddle.

INSIDER'S TIP CHECK OUT THE EXCITING ROTATION OF GUEST BEANS BEING BREWED IN THE CHEMEX

Lazy lunches and afternoon sugar-fixes – courtesy of Brown & Blonde bakery – are followed by espresso martinis (you'll find the same intense Dark Arches blend that worked so well with milk, killing it in the cocktail), craft beers and bites after dark. And in summer, we'd recommend arriving early to bag yourself a spot in the garden that's festooned with fairy lights.

On the first Sunday of every month, the Social teams up with other indie businesses in Fossgate for a street festival with food, drink and live music.

KEY ROASTER
North Star

BREWING METHODS
Espresso,
Chemex

MACHINE
La Marzocco
Linea

GRINDERS
Mazzer Super Jolly,
Mini Electronic

OPENING HOURS
Mon-Thu
8.30am-12am
Fri 8.30am-12.30am
Sat 9am-12.30am
Sun 10am-11pm

 Gluten FREE

 COFFEE BEANS AVAILABLE

 SOYA MILK AVAILABLE

 WIFI

 CYCLE FRIENDLY

 OUTDOOR SEATING

DISABLED ACCESS

 DOG FRIENDLY

www.thefossgatesocial.com T: 07979 911234
f the fossgate SOCIAL 🐦 @fossgatesocial 📷 @fossgatesocial

No. 41. SPRING ESPRESSO

45 Fossgate, York, North Yorkshire, YO1 9TF.

Stepping into Spring Espresso in Fossgate, you wouldn't realise you were in a UKBC sensory judge's coffee shop – until you have a coffee.

Because there's no daunting snobbery here, just a mix of locals catching up with friends over flat whites, caffeine fiends sipping Small Batch coffee made in the AeroPress, and people tucking into bacon and maple pancake stacks in this airy space.

INSIDER'S TIP STEVE ALSO JUDGES THE UK LATTE ART AND UK COFFEE IN GOOD SPIRITS COMPS

Square Mile's seasonal blend is lovingly crafted into espresso on the Synesso Hydra machine by owner Steve Dyson and his brigade of baristas, with guest coffee roasters such as Workshop, Nude and Caravan always available, too. In summer make sure to ask for the 12 hour cold brew behind the bar that's just waiting to be slurped with tonic.

Food-wise, the options are as inspiring as the coffee, with breakfast served all day and plenty of panini and other carby goodies to enjoy ... pastrami, mustard mayo and pickle bagel? Bring it on.

KEY ROASTER
Square Mile

BREWING METHODS
Espresso, V60, AeroPress, cold brew

MACHINE
Synesso Hydra

GRINDERS
Mythos One, Clima Pro

OPENING HOURS
Mon-Sun
8am-6pm

www.springespresso.co.uk   T: 07779 294149

f Spring Espresso   🐦 @springespresso   📷 @springespresso

№42. WESTMORELAND COFFEE

2 Westmoreland Street, Harrogate, North Yorkshire, HG1 5AT.

Starting with a small take-out espresso bar in 2014, Jamie Marlow soon realised he was going to need bigger digs to meet the demand for quality coffee in this residential area of Harrogate.

Opening a couple of doors down in August 2015, Westmoreland enjoys a bright and uncluttered space in which to unwind and enjoy great coffee and good company, thanks to the eclectic mix of art and reclaimed furniture, high ceilings and panoramic views.

INSIDER'S TIP: THE TRIPLE CHOCOLATE BROWNIE SERVED WITH PISTACHIO AFFOGATO IS NOT TO BE MISSED

'The interior probably reflects the Londoner in me,' explains Jamie, whose passion for the bean was ignited in his student days spent hopping coffee bars in the capital, and continued to smoulder in the three years he spent living in New York and LA. 'Some coffee bars overcomplicate what makes a good cup, but I've learnt to teach our baristas to simply make the most of each coffee's unique flavours,' he says.

A drool-worthy line-up of gourmet sandwiches is the icing on the cake at this lively hangout - and yep, they serve a good slice of that too.

KEY ROASTER
North Star

BREWING METHODS
Espresso, V60, AeroPress

MACHINE
La Spaziale S5

GRINDER
Sanremo SR70

OPENING HOURS
Mon-Fri 8.30am-5pm
Sat 9am-5pm
Sun 9am-2pm

T: 01423 562918

f Westmoreland Speciality Coffee 🐦 @westmorelandcfe 📷 @westmorelandspecialitycoffee

№ 43. BEAN AND BUD

14 Commercial Street, Harrogate, North Yorkshire, HG1 1TY.

After five years' experience working with coffee farmers, it's no surprise to find that Ruth Hampson, the co-owner of Bean and Bud, has introduced the kind of commitment to provenance of beans to this cafe that you'd usually find at a top grade roastery.

Cosying up with local roasters Dark Woods, the team enjoys a privileged pick of the Yorkshire roastery's micro-lots, which can be enjoyed in a range of brewing methods from the well-equipped bar.

If you like what you're drinking, we'd suggest you get the coffees in while you can, as the single origins change as frequently as the tempting lunch offerings – there's a range of speciality roasters to choose from on the chalk boards.

Sarnies, cakes and bakes to be scoffed alongside a killer cup are sourced with the same eye for ethics and quality credentials as the coffee, with Ruth using gluten-free, organic and local ingredients in her homemade goodies, wherever possible.

KEY ROASTERS
Dark Woods,
Round Hill Roastery,
The Barn

BREWING METHODS
Espresso, V60,
Chemex,
AeroPress, syphon

MACHINE
La Marzocco Strada

GRINDERS
Mythos One,
Mahlkonig K30,
Tanzania

OPENING HOURS
Mon-Sat
8am-5pm

INSIDER'S TIP WANT TO TAKE YOUR MILK SKILLS TO INSTAGRAM-WORTHY HEIGHTS? LOOK OUT FOR BEAN AND BUD'S LATTE ART COURSES

www.beanandbud.co.uk   T: 01423 508200

f Bean & Bud   🐦 @beanandbud   📷 @beanandbud

44. BALTZERSEN'S

22 Oxford Street, Harrogate, North Yorkshire, HG1 1PU.

From interiors to eating habits to our coffee rituals, you'll have to have been living under a rock to not notice the influence of Scandi style lately. But it was actually fond memories of his Norwegian grandmother, Liv Esther Baltzersen, and her traditional Nordic cooking that inspired Paul Rawlinson to open a Scandinavian cafe in the centre of Harrogate in 2012.

You could easily lose a whole day at this spacious hangout; starting early with Scandi staples such as skyr and pyttipanne (Swedish bubble and squeak), moseying to mid-morning with North Star's bespoke espresso blend and freshly baked cinnamon buns, breezing through lunch feasting on traditional smørbrød (open sandwiches) and, finally, fuelling the afternoon with fruit topped waffles and single origin bulk brew from Maude Coffee Roasters.

To top it off, you'll discover a troupe of friendly staff knocking about to keep you company, too, who love coffee and good food as much as you. Sweet.

KEY ROASTER
North Star

BREWING METHODS
Espresso,
bulk brew,
AeroPress

MACHINE
La Spaziale S5

GRINDERS
Mahlkonig K30 Air,
Mahlkonig EK43

OPENING HOURS
Mon-Sat 8am-5pm
Sun 10am-4pm

INSIDER'S TIP BY EVENING, BALTZERSEN'S TRANSFORMS INTO A LAID-BACK FINE DINING RESTAURANT CALLED NORSE

www.baltzersens.co.uk   T: 01423 202363

f Baltzersens   🐦 @baltzersens   📷 @baltzersens

№45. HOXTON NORTH

52 Parliament Street, Harrogate, North Yorkshire, HG1 2RL.

A unique mashup of speciality grade coffee, boutique wines, craft beers and London-inspired homewares, Hoxton North is a hangout for the aspirational.

Everything in this creative space has been selected with great care and attention by owners Timothy and Victoria Bosworth, from the lengthy list of roasters - Nude, Origin and Allpress to name a few - to the indie magazines and newspapers scattered along the central brew bar.

INSIDER'S TIP YOU'LL FIND PLENTY OF VEGAN, DAIRY AND GLUTEN FREE TREATS, PLUS AN IMPRESSIVE RANGE OF BIODYNAMIC WINES AND CRAFT BEERS

Dark wood, vintage mirrors and French cafe tables add a European feel to the Grade II-listed building, making it the kind of place where you can spend a few hours mulling over ideas with a flat white and a handmade pastry, or a fave spot for post work drinks on a Friday evening.

Browse Hoxton North's intriguing range of accessories and homewares in situ or get your shopping fix out-of-hours through its online store.

KEY ROASTERS
Multiple

BREWING METHODS
Espresso, AeroPress, V60, Chemex

MACHINE
La Marzocco GB/5

GRINDERS
Mazzer on demand, Mahlkonig

OPENING HOURS
Mon-Wed 8.30am-5pm
Thu-Fri 8.30am-9pm
Sat 9.30am-9pm
Sun 10am-4pm

Gluten FREE
COFFEE BEANS AVAILABLE
SOYA MILK AVAILABLE
WIFI
CYCLE FRIENDLY
OUTDOOR SEATING
FAMILY FRIENDLY

www.hoxtonnorth.com
f Hoxton North @hoxtonnorth @hoxtonnorth

№46. THE HEDGEROW

Station Road, Threshfield, North Yorkshire, BD23 5BP.

Wendy Hutchinson never planned to run a cafe. In fact, The Hedgerow opened as a florist shop in 1993, but over the past two decades it's blossomed into a coffee shop, flower school and pop-up event venue.

It was when Wendy's daughter Heather joined the team in 2014 that the coffee side of the business was kicked up a few levels, inspired by her time studying in London coffee shops.

INSIDER'S TIP — IF THE SUN'S SHINING, TREAT YOURSELF TO A GLASS OF PROSECCO IN THE COURTYARD

Now you'll find Atkinson's speciality beans doing the business as house roast and Lonton and Coopers Coffee making regular guest appearances on filter.

A good bunch of homemade bakes makes sticking around to enjoy the coffee in-house all the more tempting, and sitting among scented swathes of fresh flowers that are delivered daily from Holland is an added bonus.

KEY ROASTER
J. Atkinson & Co.

BREWING METHODS
Espresso, filter

MACHINE
Nuova Simonelli

GRINDER
Mythos

OPENING HOURS
Mon-Fri 9am-5pm
Sat 9am-4pm

 Gluten FREE

 COFFEE BEANS AVAILABLE

 SOYA MILK AVAILABLE

 WIFI

 CYCLE FRIENDLY

 OUTDOOR SEATING

 COFFEE COURSES AVAILABLE

 FAMILY FRIENDLY

 DISABLED ACCESS

DOG FRIENDLY

www.the-hedgerow.co.uk T: 01756 752293

f The Hedgerow, Threshfield 🐦 @hedgerowflorist 📷 @the_hedgerow

№ 47. BEAN LOVED COFFEE BAR

17 Otley Street, Skipton, North Yorkshire, BD23 1DY.

Run by talented father and son team of Steve and Wes Bond, Bean Loved is a well-established coffee institution in the heart of Skipton.

Very much a locals' coffee shop, it was opened nine years ago in a former tea room and, ever since, the family duo has been flying the flag for speciality coffee, garnering a loyal band of regulars who pop in at all times of the day for their coffee fix.

INSIDER'S TIP THE TEAS FROM CANTON TEA ARE PRETTY SPECIAL

Steve developed his love of the bean after spending 10 years as a coffee sales manager. This was backed up by Wes' travels in New Zealand and Australia where, working as a barista, he got to learn about the speciality scene.

And now the pair have a long standing relationship with Yorkshire roaster Grumpy Mule which creates the house signature blend. The accompanying food is superb - an ever changing range of fabulous cakes, including gluten-free options and inspired salads (poached pear, gorgonzola, walnut, beetroot puree and pancetta anyone?) and brunch options.

KEY ROASTER
Grumpy Mule

BREWING METHOD
Espresso

MACHINE
La Marzocco FB80

GRINDERS
Mythos One,
Mahlkonig EK43

OPENING HOURS
Mon-Fri
7.30am-5pm
Sat 8am-5pm
Sun 9am-5pm

Gluten FREE

COFFEE BEANS AVAILABLE

SOYA MILK AVAILABLE

WIFI

CYCLE FRIENDLY

OUTDOOR SEATING

FAMILY FRIENDLY

DISABLED ACCESS

www.beanloved.co.uk T: 01756 791534

f Bean Loved 🐦 @beanloved 📷 @beanloved

48. TOAST HOUSE

22 Leeds Road, Ilkley, Leeds, West Yorkshire, LS29 8DS.

It wasn't a pure passion for coffee but a love of baking, design and toast (surprise, surprise) that inspired Natasha Byers and Lisa Jenkins to open Toast House in Ilkley.

With a keen eye for interiors, the duo wasted no time getting to work re-upholstering, repairing and bargain hunting all the furniture for this quirky coffee shop, when they got the keys in 2013.

A zeal for the dark stuff soon followed, and after weeks of studying, the team at Toast quickly learnt to deliver the perfect shot every time with beans sourced from J. Atkinson and Co. and North Star. You can buy a bag to-go too, if you discover a new gem used in your morning flat white.

When it comes to feasting, it's all about the unsung breakfast hero – yep, toast – at this welcoming hangout. We're not talking run-of-the-mill white sliced though, this is the worship of slowly proved, chewy, richly crusted sourdough toast, topped with melting butter and top quality preserves. Later in the day, eat it smothered in avocado, topped with tangy tomato or dipped into chunky soup.

KEY ROASTER
J. Atkinson & Co.

BREWING METHOD
Espresso

MACHINE
La Spaziale

GRINDER
Mazzer

OPENING HOURS
Mon-Fri 9am-4pm
Sat 9am-5pm

Gluten FREE

COFFEE BEANS AVAILABLE

SOYA MILK AVAILABLE

WIFI

INSIDER'S TIP POP UP FOOD AND COFFEE EVENTS ARE IN THE PIPELINE THIS YEAR

www.toasthouse.co.uk T: 01943 601987
f Toast House Ilkley 🐦 @toastilkley 📷 @toastilkley

№49. BOWERY

54 Otley Road, Headingley, Leeds, West Yorkshire, LS6 2AL.

A gallery, design studio, workshop and cafe, Bowery in Leeds is a creative hub where the community's plethora of passions come together under one roof and - luckily for us all - that also includes coffee.

The cafe is at the heart of this artistic space and alongside fresh, seasonal salads, Bondgate Bakery quiches and delicious homemade cakes, you'll find a sterling cup of AllPress Espresso's Redchurch blend on hand to keep those creative juices flowing.

INSIDER'S TIP THE BANANA AND WALNUT LOAF IS A MUST AT ANY TIME OF THE DAY

And when head barista Ged Togher isn't pulling shots for punters, he's teaching tomorrow's baristas the coffee craft. Held on the last Thursday of every month, Bowery's beginner's coffee classes are designed to show home brewing enthusiasts how to make the most of their machine – from the perfect grind to the swishest latte art.

KEY ROASTER
Allpress Espresso

BREWING METHOD
Espresso

MACHINE
CMA Gloria Astoria

GRINDER
Mazzer Super Jolly

OPENING HOURS
Mon-Thu
9am-6.30pm
Fri-Sat
9am-6pm
Sun 10am-5pm

www.thebowery.org   T: 01132 242284

f Bowery   🐦 @theboweryarts   📷 @boweryleeds

№50. OPPOSITE – CHAPEL ALLERTON

4 Stainbeck Lane, Chapel Allerton, Leeds, West Yorkshire, LS7 3QY.

You'll have to work for your coffee and search this one out, as Opposite's newest hangout is currently incognito – bare-faced and unbranded.

Snugly located between the pharmacy and bank, the Chapel Allerton venue upholds family tradition with a solid bill of Square Mile espresso-based drinks (as well as AeroPress and bulk brew) and a friendly bunch of baristas behind the bar.

INSIDER'S TIP MAKE YOURSELF AT HOME AND THINK OF THIS NEIGHBOURHOOD CAFF AS AN EXTENSION OF YOUR LIVING ROOM

Do visit armed with an appetite, as once you've scoffed sourdough toast, homemade granola and smoked salmon and cream cheese at brunch, you'll probably want to stick around for hearty salads, superlative sarnies and chunky soups for a late lunch.

When the sun's out, there's a spacious outdoor seating area in which to enjoy a cake and coffee (including guest North Star roasts), while in colder months there's plenty of room to kick back in the homely wood-panelled interior.

KEY ROASTER
Square Mile

BREWING METHODS
Espresso, AeroPress, bulk brew

MACHINE
Synesso Hydra

GRINDER
Mythos One

OPENING HOURS
Mon–Fri 7am-6pm
Sat 8am-6pm
Sun 9am-5pm

Gluten FREE

COFFEE BEANS AVAILABLE

SOYA MILK AVAILABLE

WIFI

OUTDOOR seating

FAMILY FRIENDLY

DISABLED ACCESS

DOG FRIENDLY

---

www.oppositecafe.co.uk

No.51. HOUSE OF KOKO

62 Harrogate Road, Chapel Allerton, Leeds, West Yorkshire, LS7 4LA.

This gorgeous little cafe in north Leeds not only offers top notch coffee, it's also a go-to place for speciality teas, inspiring food and a very jolly atmosphere.

It was set up by Shanshan Zhu and Chris Ball, with Shanshan responsible for the look of the place – it's bright, colourful and decked out with retro furnishings and geometric patterns – as well as the feel, and by this we mean the happy and very warm welcome, whether you're a regular or visiting for the first time.

Coming from an IT background, this is the couple's first foodie venture and it's already a success. *The reaction has been phenomenal, far exceeding our expectations,'* says Chris.

INSIDER'S TIP ITS POP UP RESTAURANT NIGHTS ARE HOSTING SOME OF THE REGION'S UP-AND-COMING CHEFS

This is partly due to the quality drinks – they use Leeds roaster North Star - as well as the attention to food. You'll find an excellent selection of panini and platters (a fave is the bacon baked beans on sourdough) and an inspired cake offering – dandelion and burdock anyone? Chris says there are now plans afoot to develop the coffee shop further – you heard it here first.

KEY ROASTER
North Star

BREWING METHODS
Espresso, V60

MACHINE
Astoria Gloria AL3 3 group, lever-operated

GRINDER
Mazzer

OPENING HOURS
Mon-Fri 8am-6pm
Sat 9am-5pm
Sun 10am-4pm

www.houseofkoko.com T: 01132 621808

f House of Koko   @houseofkoko   @houseofkoko

52. CAFE 164

Munro House, Duke Street, Leeds, West Yorkshire, LS9 8AG.

Hot from the roaring success of Bakery 164, with its famed, freshly-baked ciabatta and focaccia, comes sister venture, Cafe 164.

If the bakery is a feast of all things carby, this is a chance for the team to focus on coffee – with those gorgeous baked goodies on the side.

Sourcing independent and local artisan roasters is key here and they keep it local with a main coffee supplier of North Star of Leeds. But just as man cannot live on bread alone, both house and guest beans are regularly rotated with Maude, Casa Espresso and Dark Woods beans – to name but a few.

All this is served in the lovely setting of The Gallery at Munro House, which is an exhibition and event space, showing work from artists as well as providing a pop up venue for live music and supper clubs.

KEY ROASTER
North Star

BREWING METHODS
Espresso, filter

MACHINE
La Marzocco

GRINDERS
Mazzer Luigi,
Sanremo

OPENING HOURS
Mon-Fri 8am-6pm
Sat 10am-6pm

Gluten FREE

COFFEE BEANS AVAILABLE

SOYA MILK AVAILABLE

WIFI

INSIDER'S TIP CAFE 164 IS HOME TO LEEDS' COFFEE SOCIAL WHICH SHOWCASES THE CITY'S INDIE COFFEE SCENE

www.cafe164.com T: 01132 433266
f Cafe 164 @cafe164 @cafe164

№53. KAPOW! COFFEE

44 The Calls, Leeds, West Yorkshire, LS2 7EW.

The creative workforce who spend their nine to five at The Calls have struck it lucky having Kapow! Coffee on their patch, just seconds away from the River Aire.

Packed out with locals craving a caffeine fix first thing, and again during its cheeky happy hour between 10-11, swinging by for a coffee-to-go at this pocket sized spot is a must on this side of town.

INSIDER'S TIP WHEN IT'S HOT, ASK THE GUYS FOR AN AFFOGATO SERVED WITH NORTHERN BLOC ICE CREAM

Beans come courtesy of La Bottega Milanese, with guest appearances from a number of other local roasters. The guys have just installed a nitro machine from Artemis too, so visitors can enjoy cold brew as well as the line up of espresso-based drinks on the Sanremo machine.

You'll find a selection of locally sourced tray bakes and pastries on the bar if your coffee's looking lonely, along with sandwiches and savoury bites. And if you're lucky, you'll be able to pinch one of the colourful stools at the window to take a little time over your cup.

KEY ROASTER
La Bottega Milanese

BREWING METHODS
Espresso, nitro cold brew

MACHINE
Sanremo

GRINDER
Sanremo

OPENING HOURS
Mon-Fri
7.30am-4pm
Sat 9am-4pm

 COFFEE BEANS AVAILABLE

 SOYA MILK AVAILABLE

 DISABLED ACCESS

 CYCLE FRIENDLY

 DOG FRIENDLY

f Kapow Coffee   🐦 @kapowcoffee   📷 @kapowcoffee

№54. CIELO - DUNCAN STREET

7 Duncan Street, Leeds, West Yorkshire, LS1 6DQ.

With three of the four Cielo clan in Leeds, the Duncan Street venue should be your pick for a little coffee calm in the centre of the city.

Perched just a few feet from one of Leeds' busiest shopping streets, the small but perfectly formed cafe is the ideal spot to take five and refuel before returning to battle with the bargain hunters.

Roasting its own beans at its sister-venue in Garforth, the coffee's fragrantly fresh, and with brewing options such as V60, AeroPress and syphon, there's reason to take a little more time over the goods in a filter.

INSIDER'S TIP LOOK OUT FOR FREE COFFEE TASTING EVENTS AND BREWING DEMONSTRATIONS

Brewing tips and tasting notes from the latest seasonal blend are always just a question away too, with baristas Matt and Hollie always up for a spot of coffee chat.

As well as donating its profits to help the community flourish, Cielo also supports local musicians and creatives, so keep an eye on social media for pop up events – and don't be surprised if you're greeted with a few chords on the guitar.

KEY ROASTER
Cielo Coffee Roasters

BREWING METHODS
Espresso, V60, AeroPress, syphon

MACHINE
La Marzocco Strada EP

GRINDER
Mythos One

OPENING HOURS
Mon-Fri
8am-5.30pm
Sat 9am-5pm
Sun 11am-5pm

 Gluten FREE

 COFFEE BEANS AVAILABLE

 SOYA MILK AVAILABLE

 WIFI

 OUTDOOR SEATING

 COFFEE COURSES AVAILABLE

 FAMILY FRIENDLY

 DISABLED ACCESS

www.cielouk.com T: 01132 438537

f Cielo Coffee Duncan St 🐦 @cielouk 📷 @cielocoffee

55. OPPOSITE

MAP

Queen Victoria Street, Leeds, West Yorkshire, LS1 6AZ.

Proving that size isn't everything, Opposite in Victoria Quarter may be one of the country's teeniest coffee spots, but this hasn't stopped the team cranking out some of the best speciality coffee around.

INSIDER'S TIP PINCH A SPOT BY THE FOUNTAINS AND GRAB A REJUVENATING COFFEE BETWEEN SHOPS

With an old-school set up in the centre of a Victorian arcade, Opposite's second venue in the city fuels busy shoppers with a small but sturdy line-up of espresso-based drinks from the kiosk's Synesso machine. Square Mile is the roaster of choice but when the baristas spy something truly tasty, regulars can enjoy a guest espresso from the likes of North Star and Has Bean through the Anfim grinder.

Homemade cakes, savoury snacks and its famous (in Leeds, anyway) chocolate brownies make a good match for the coffee, and are all made by hand at one of Opposite's sister venues. You won't find any additives, preservatives or similar stuff in its bakes either, just a whole lotta love – and a fair few calories. There's also a range of brewing gear and beans available to buy to stock up your home brew bar.

KEY ROASTER
Square Mile

BREWING METHOD
Espresso

MACHINE
Synesso

GRINDER
Anfim

OPENING HOURS
Mon-Fri 9am-5pm
Sat 9am-6pm
Sun 10am-5pm

 Gluten FREE

 COFFEE BEANS AVAILABLE

 SOYA MILK AVAILABLE

 OUTDOOR seating

 DISABLED ACCESS

 DOG FRIENDLY

www.oppositecafe.co.uk

f Opposite Cafe   🐦 @oppositecafe   📷 @oppositecafe

56. LA BOTTEGA MILANESE

2 Bond Court, Leeds, West Yorkshire, LS1 2JZ.

'*The Italian espresso bar is a social affair, the embodiment of continental cafe culture,*' says Alex Galantino, the founder of the north of England's most authentic slice of Italy.

And he should know, having been so inspired while working at Milanese espresso bars in his home country, that he was compelled to launch a fusion concept of Italian purist techniques and third wave best practice in Leeds. '*Our objective is to recreate the Milanese coffee bar experience, brick for brick, from ambience to product,*' he says.

For Italians, only the best will do when it comes to food and coffee, and it's exactly the same at La Bottega, where the team uses artisan-roasted beans from Dark Woods for the house espresso, along with a full selection of guest roasts from other leading UK roasters.

Fine cured meats, cheeses and seriously good patisserie come direct from Italy, while pasta and cakes are made by local Italian chefs. And everything that's not from Italy is from Yorkshire, including organic milk and bread from a local co-operative.

There's a little upgrade too this year, as the cafe's recently got a full licence, so get ready for a late afternoon aperitivo in the sun.

KEY ROASTER
Dark Woods

BREWING METHODS
Espresso,
Marco Shuttle,
AeroPress, V60

MACHINES
KWDW Mirage,
LM Linea

GRINDERS
Mythos,
Cimbali Magnum,
Tanzania

OPENING HOURS
Mon-Fri 7am-6pm
Sat 9am-6pm
Sun 10am-5pm

COFFEE BEANS AVAILABLE

SOYA MILK AVAILABLE

WIFI

CYCLE FRIENDLY

OUTDOOR seating

COFFEE COURSES AVAILABLE

DISABLED ACCESS

INSIDER'S TIP JOIN THE STAFF ON SUNDAY MORNINGS FOR CUPPING SESSIONS

www.labottegamilanese.co.uk   T: 01132 431102

f La Bottega Milanese   🐦 @bottegamilanese   ✉ @labottegamilanese

57. LAYNES ESPRESSO

16 New Station Street, Leeds, West Yorkshire, LS1 5DL.

Since it opened in 2011, Laynes has become a "name" across the North - and beyond - for its great coffee. There's always a rotating offer of both espresso and brewed speciality coffee on the menu, and not only does the coffee taste great, it also demonstrates a level of consistency and quality that's difficult to achieve.

INSIDER'S TIP LAYNES WAS ONE OF THE FIRST SHOPS TO OFFER A SPLIT SHOT ON ITS MENU

It all stems from the high standards of founder, Dave Olejnik - and his team certainly doesn't let him down. It also explains why Laynes has become a go-to place for all things coffee, including advice on buying beans, brewing and training.

And help is just as available to the home brew crowd as businesses. *'We offer training to both home users who want more knowledge and a chance to use the sort of top end equipment that Laynes baristas use day in, day out, as well as to businesses who are starting up or want further insight into the world of speciality coffee,'* says Dave.

And while you're mulling over brewing techniques, indulge in the small, but perfectly formed, sandwich or breakfast menus.

KEY ROASTER
Square Mile

BREWING METHODS
Espresso, V60, AeroPress

MACHINE
Victoria Arduino
Black Eagle
Gravitech

GRINDER
Mythos One

OPENING HOURS
Mon-Fri 7am-7pm
Sat 9am-6pm
Sun 10am-5pm

Gluten FREE

---

www.laynesespresso.co.uk T: 07828 823189

f Laynes Espresso 🐦 @laynesespresso ✉ @laynesespresso

58. OUT OF THE WOODS

Watermans Place, Wharf Approach, Leeds, West Yorkshire, LS1 4GL.

Emerge from the southern exit of Leeds train station and you'll find yourself in a sylvan woodland with squirrels darting across the wallpaper and peeping from behind trays of caramel shortbread. Don't be concerned, you HAVE arrived in the gritty metropolis of Leeds, you've just made a detour via Ross Stringer's Out Of The Woods cafe.

INSIDER'S TIP: TRY THE ACAI BOWL OF FRESH BERRIES WITH CRUNCHY GRANOLA AND BANANA

Good coffee is as beneficial to the soul as time spent in nature, so Ross' use of beans roasted by Dark Woods in Marsden makes this a replenishing experience. Meanwhile, the body is taken care of with healthy and delicious smoothies, salads and sandwiches, which are all freshly made on the premises with new specials every few days. And while the salted caramel millionaire's shortbread may not be essential for health, it'll certainly make you happy.

With waterfront views of the canal and a lovely warm welcome by knowledgeable and friendly staff, discover a little grove of delight.

KEY ROASTER
Dark Woods

BREWING METHOD
Espresso

MACHINE
La Spaziale

GRINDER
Mahlkonig K30

OPENING HOURS
Mon-Fri 7am-4pm
Sat 8.30am-2.30pm
Closed at 3pm
in winter

Gluten FREE

COFFEE BEANS AVAILABLE

SOYA MILK AVAILABLE

WIFI

CYCLE FRIENDLY

OUTDOOR SEATING

DISABLED ACCESS

www.outofthewoods.me.uk   T: 01132 454144

f Out of the Woods   @outofthewoodsuk   @outofthewoodsuk

№59. OUT OF THE WOODS – WATER LANE

113 Water Lane, Leeds, West Yorkshire, LS11 5WD.

Get ready for a blast of nature at Out Of The Woods, the quirky cafe in the centre of regenerated Holbeck Urban Village.

Astro turf outside, squirrels hiding in the wallpaper and on mugs, and Dark Woods coffee make this a rejuvenating place to enjoy an espresso-based coffee and something good to eat.

INSIDER'S TIP LET THE OUT OF THE WOODS CREW DELIVER LUNCH TO YOUR OFFICE FOR YOUR NEXT MEETING

Visit for the scrumptious breakfast menu crammed with thick-cut toasties, rustic granola and fruit-packed smoothies.

Worker bees from the surrounding funky business park mingle with coffee lovers who make a visit to this part of the city just for a quality cup.

It's no surprise, as Out Of The Woods owner Ross and her team are serious about creating a great cafe experience, using local suppliers from across the county, grinding beans on demand for freshness, and sourcing local, organic milk. The signature sandwich list is lovely and there's a natural emphasis on the homemade.

KEY ROASTER
Dark Woods

BREWING METHOD
Espresso

MACHINE
DeLatte

GRINDER
Mahlkonig K30

OPENING HOURS
Mon-Fri
7am-4pm
Closed at 3pm
in winter

www.outofthewoods.me.uk T: 01132 448123

Out of the Woods @outofthewoodsuk @outofthewoodsuk

60. CIELO - GARFORTH

41 Main Street, Garforth, Leeds, West Yorkshire, LS25 1DS.

Delicious coffee is so much sweeter when you know that your hard earned pennies are going straight back into the community, so you won't be needing sugar at Cielo in Garforth.

Born out of Nick and Linda Castle's desire for change, the cafe was set up as a speciality coffee roaster come social hub in 2008. Growing in popularity, Cielo quickly outgrew its original home on Main Street, but its mission to reduce loneliness and support local businesses burns on in its new, roomier roost down the road.

INSIDER'S TIP: ALL CIELO'S PROFITS GO TO LOCAL COMMUNITY GROUPS

When it comes to spreading community spirit, we reckon coffee's a good place to start, and roasting its own speciality blend on site, Cielo's got a lot of love to give.

Take time to sample the house beans fresh from the grinder, as the friendly staff – many of whom are volunteers – are more than happy to chat coffee, plus there are tasty snacks to get your chops around, too.

KEY ROASTER
Cielo Coffee Roasters

BREWING METHODS
Espresso, V60

MACHINE
La Marzocco GB80

GRINDER
Mahlkonig K30

OPENING HOURS
Mon-Fri
8.45am-5pm
Sat-Sun
9.30am-4pm

www.cielouk.com   T: 01132 863534

f Cielo Coffee   🐦 @cielouk   📷 @cielocoffee

61. COFFEEVOLUTION

8 Church Street, Huddersfield, West Yorkshire, HD1 1DD.

O pening Huddersfield's first espresso bar way-back-when in the year 2000, owner Jeremy Perkins was no doubt a key influencer in the speciality coffee scene which has spread across this historic market town.

INSIDER'S TIP **WING BY ON THE FIRST SUNDAY OF EACH MONTH FOR AN EPIC BRUNCH SESSION FEATURING FRENCH TOAST, WAFFLES AND A FULL VEGAN BREKKIE**

It was touring the world as a professional viola player that inspired Jeremy's interest in the dark stuff, and it's an enticing blend of his two passions which makes Coffeevolution unique. Because, in addition to cranking out top notch brews using beans from Jeremy and his brother James' roastery, Bean Brothers Coffee Company – alongside an impressive list of guest roasts – the cafe also hosts a creative calendar of art, music and theatre events.

Discover a solid line-up of lunchtime staples for hungry caffeine tourists: bagels, salads, grilled cheese – you know the drill, and a selection of enticing cakes and sweet treats baked by sister, Sally.

KEY ROASTER
Bean Brothers
Coffee Company

BREWING METHODS
Espresso,
AeroPress,
V60, Chemex,
cold brew, nitro

MACHINE
La Marzocco FB80

GRINDERS
Mazzer, Anfim

OPENING HOURS
Mon-Fri 7am-7pm
Sat 7.30am-7pm
Sun 9am-6pm

www.coffeevolution.co.uk   T: 01484 432881

f Coffeevolution Huddersfield   🐦 @coffeevolution   ✉ @coffeevolutionhuddersfield

№62. THE COFFEEKABIN

35-37 Queensgate, Huddersfield, West Yorkshire, HD1 2RD.

Drawing customers from miles around, the Coffeekabin is a winning mix of food, drink and Yorkshire hospitality.

Near the university in Queensgate, and now into its second year, The Coffeekabin was set up by Simon Frewin. He'd got the coffee bug while playing professional rugby in New Zealand and, on coming home, launched a coffee van, before moving to his permanent shop location.

INSIDER'S TIP VISIT FOR THE THEMED EVENINGS WHERE FOOD, BEER, WINE AND COFFEE ARE MATCHED

Simon is meticulous about coffee, rotating two espressos and one filter, and brewing to perfection. And he pays as much attention to Coffeekabin's other offerings, including 15 loose leaf teas from Canton and a carefully selected range of eight wines and 11 craft beers (which you can also take away). There are gins and whiskies available, too.

What's more, such has been the success of the food offering, that Simon now has two talented chefs working with him, creating bistro menus featuring choices from brioche bun gourmet burgers to slow braised lamb shoulder with celeriac mash.

KEY ROASTER
Origin Coffee

BREWING METHODS
Espresso, V60, AeroPress, Chemex

MACHINE
La Marzocco Strada

GRINDERS
Mythos, Mahlkonig EK43

OPENING HOURS
Mon-Wed
8am-5pm
Thu-Sat
8am-10pm

www.thecoffeekabin.com   T: 07980 373699

f The Coffeekabin   @thecoffeekabin   @thecoffeekabino

N° 63. THE HANDMADE BAKERY

Unit 6, Upper Mills, Canal Side, Slaithwaite, Huddersfield, West Yorkshire, HD7 5HA.

This thriving bakery in a former weaving shed, right beside the Huddersfield Narrow Canal in Slaithwaite, is a must-visit.

Not only for the seductive aroma of freshly baked bread and pastries to tempt you every morning, but also to track down a quality cup of speciality coffee made using beans from local roastery, Dark Woods.

It scores 100 per cent for feel-good factor in other ways too, as the bakery was set up as a workers' co-operative and consequently has a strong, ethical core that gives everyone who brews, bakes or visits here, a genuine sense of heartwarming pride.

INSIDER'S TIP DON'T MISS ITS FAMOUS SAVOURY DANISH PASTRIES

Lively and sociable, there's a constant buzz of activity (it turns out over 1,500 bakery items every week) and it's a popular port of call for families, cyclists and foodies alike. A big draw is being able to sit back and watch the bakers at work. Of course the downside of this is that you'll find it nearly impossible to leave without eating something from the stunning patisserie range, or a lunch adorned with fresh herbs and salad leaves straight from the kitchen garden.

KEY ROASTER
Dark Woods

BREWING METHOD
Espresso

MACHINE
Sanremo

GRINDER
Sanremo SR50A

OPENING HOURS
Tue-Sun
9.30am-4.30pm

 Gluten FREE

 COFFEE BEANS AVAILABLE

 SOYA MILK AVAILABLE

 WIFI

 CYCLE FRIENDLY

 OUTDOOR SEATING

FAMILY FRIENDLY

DISABLED ACCESS

www.thehandmadebakery.coop   T: 01484 842175

f The Handmade Bakery   🐦 @handmadebakery   📷 @thehandmadebakery

SOUTH YORKSHIRE
& LINCOLNSHIRE

No. 64. THE DEPOT BAKERY

92 Burton Road, Sheffield, South Yorkshire, S3 8DA.

Tamper Coffee customers have been enjoying the fruits of sister company, Depot Bakery's labours for some time now, but Depot's move from pure bakehouse at Arundel Street to its own cafe-come-bakery at Kelham Island is carb-tastic for everyone in this part of the city.

Visit for great coffee and a delicious interplay between the rough and ready industrial warehouse in which it's now housed, and the oozing, exquisite patisserie on display, ready to tempt anyone who ventured in for just a coffee.

We'd suggest you give in and grab a place at one of the communal tables for a Hodson blend filter with ham-hock eggs benedict and a crisp-out-of-the-oven pastry.

An all-day brunch menu is complemented by great bread (naturally), sarnies, pies and salads, and you can take the experience further by visiting during evening events such as the regular street food market.

KEY ROASTER
Ozone Coffee
Roasters

BREWING METHODS
Espresso,
Bunn bulk brew

MACHINE
La Marzocco
Linea

GRINDER
Mazzer Kony

OPENING HOURS
Mon-Fri 9am-3pm
Sat-Sun 9am-4pm

 INSIDER'S TIP TRY THE PERFECT PAIRING OF A FRUITY FILTER COFFEE AND A MANGO AND PASSION FRUIT DOUGHNUT

www.thedepotbakery.co.uk   T: 01142 757779

f The Depot Bakery   🐦 @thedepotbakery   📷 @thedepotbakery

65. UPSHOT ESPRESSO

355 Glossop Road, Sheffield, South Yorkshire, S10 2HP.

This busy little indie in the middle of university-land has taken off big time since last year's guide.

The core speciality coffee offering has been joined by a second seating area, mini bookshop and an expanded brunch menu (think rarebit with the city's classic Henderson's Relish) along with Nordic inspired dishes like salmon smørrebrød with poached duck egg on (the newly opened) Saturdays.

INSIDER'S TIP DISCOVER MICRO-LOT TEAS AND MATCHA TOO

It's a natural pairing with the Nordic influenced coffee. 'We like to explore different coffees from across the world,' says Sam, 'so for example we'll have coffee from Tim Wendelboe in Norway, Germany's The Barn, Somerset's Round Hill Roastery and Coffee Collective in Denmark.'

As you'd expect with that line up, everything is single origin (no blends) and the two espresso and filter coffees rotate all the time, as coffee seasons change around the world. Check the menu for weekly specials such as tasting flights, coffee tonics and micro-lot teas.

KEY ROASTERS
Tim Wendelboe,
The Barn,
Coffee Collective,
Round Hill
Roastery,
Square Mile

BREWING METHODS
Espresso, V60,
AeroPress,
Chemex,
batch filter

MACHINE
Faema E61

GRINDERS
Mahlkonig Peak,
Mahlkonig EK43

OPENING HOURS
Mon-Fri
8am-4.30pm
Sat 10am-3pm

---

www.upshotespresso.co.uk   T: 01142 780333

f Upshot Espresso   🐦 @upshotespresso   📷 @upshotespresso

N0. 66. TAMPER COFFEE: WESTFIELD TERRACE

9 Westfield Terrace, Sheffield, South Yorkshire, S1 4GH.

The original shop in the Tamper chain of three (the Depot Bakery was launched at Kelham Island this year), this hip coffee bar opened in 2011 with the aim of echoing the New Zealand coffee style of owner Jon Perry's homeland.

The Kiwi way is to focus on quality coffee and great food, while creating a vibe that puts a coffee shop at the heart of its local community – and Tamper does it in style.

Using an ever-changing selection of blends and single origin coffees from Ozone Coffee Roasters - including the house Tamper Blend - as both espresso and filter, it's a place to explore the world of speciality coffee.

INSIDER'S TIP TRY THE SPLIT SHOT AS AN EXCEPTIONAL WAY TO EXPERIENCE THE MANY SINGLE ORIGINS

Coffee is served in a variety of ways, so if you want to stick with a classic flat white, that's a case of "no worries", but if you want to experiment with coffee through the syphon, that's all good too.

The brews are complemented by a mini menu of freshly made sarnies, breakfast items, soups and salads.

KEY ROASTER
Ozone Coffee Roasters

BREWING METHODS
Espresso, V60, AeroPress, syphon

MACHINE
La Marzocco Linea

GRINDERS
Mythos, Mahlkonig EK43

OPENING HOURS
Mon-Fri
8am-4.30pm
Sat 9am-4pm
Sat 10am-4pm

Gluten FREE

COFFEE BEANS AVAILABLE

SOYA MILK AVAILABLE

WIFI

CYCLE FRIENDLY

COFFEE COURSES AVAILABLE

www.tampercoffee.co.uk   T: 01143 271080

f Tamper Coffee   🐦 @tampercoffee   📷 @tampercoffeewt

67. MARMADUKES CAFE DELI

22 Norfolk Row, Sheffield, South Yorkshire, S1 2PA.

Just round the corner from the Crucible and Winter Gardens in the centre of the city, Marmadukes is a delightful find for great coffee and food.

Plants, natural materials, quirky design features and colourful Moroccan-style tiles make this comfy and appealing both inside and outside, where you can sit in the warmer months.

INSIDER'S TIP VISIT ONE OF MARMADUKE'S MONTHLY BREWING WORKSHOPS

Order your espresso (Workshop's Cult of Done) served in all the regular ways from head barista Alex or let him craft you a Kalita Wave or AeroPress at the brew bar.

And while you're watching him, try and resist the plethora of artisan cakes and pastries at nose level on the counter in front of you – they're testament to the power of advertising.

As well as the sweet treats, there's a contemporary cafe menu including brunch served all day on a Sunday, so you can pep yourself up with pancakes, bacon and maple syrup – whenever you finally rise.

KEY ROASTER
Workshop

BREWING METHODS
Espresso,
Kalita Wave
AeroPress,
batch brew

MACHINE
La Marzocco
Linea PB

GRINDERS
Mazzer Robur,
Mahlkonig EK43

OPENING HOURS
Mon-Sat 9am-5pm
Sun 10am-4pm

www.marmadukescafedeli.co.uk   T: 01142 767462

f Marmadukes Cafe Deli   🐦 @marmadukescafe   ✉ @marmadukescafe

68. TAMPER COFFEE: SELLERS WHEEL

149 Arundel Street, Sheffield, South Yorkshire, S1 2NU.

It's all about the frankly fabulous Kiwi coffee experience at this cafe and coffee shop in the centre of the city's cultural industry quarter.

A vibrant re-imagining of a former silversmiths, the bare brick walls, rough hewn wooden tables and concrete floors are complemented by luscious plants tumbling from the ceilings and an exotic mural of tropical birds and flowers. More delights from hot climes come in the form of carefully hand crafted coffee in a number of serve styles, as well as house-made cold brew, iced teas and juices.

INSIDER'S TIP GET THE ULTIMATE NZ EXPERIENCE WITH A FLAT WHITE, MINCE ON TOAST AND A LAMINGTON

Quality drinks are matched by great food such as sweetcorn fritters, New Zealand lamb sarnies, vodka and beetroot-infused salmon salad, and cakes from its own bakery (and new cafe), The Depot Bakery at Kelham Island.

Start the day here with coffee and breakfast, linger on for lunch, then throw in the towel and settle in for the evening with craft beers and supper. Sweet as, bro.

KEY ROASTER
Ozone Coffee Roasters

BREWING METHODS
Espresso, pourover V60, AeroPress, cold brew

MACHINE
La Marzocco GB5

GRINDERS
Mazzer Kony, Mahlkonig EK43

OPENING HOURS
Mon-Thurs 8am-5pm
Fri 8am-10pm
Sat 9am-6pm
Sun 9am-4pm

 Gluten FREE

 COFFEE BEANS AVAILABLE

 SOYA MILK AVAILABLE

 WIFI

 CYCLE FRIENDLY

 OUTDOOR SEATING

 COFFEE COURSES AVAILABLE

 FAMILY FRIENDLY

 DISABLED ACCESS

www.tampercoffee.co.uk   T: 01142 757970

f Tamper Coffee   @tampercoffee   @tampercoffeesw

Your beverage menu requires equipment that is consistently reliable and precise. **Choose Experience. Choose BUNN.**

69. FORGE BAKEHOUSE

302 Abbeydale Road, Sheffield, South Yorkshire, S7 1FL.

This busy little sourdough bakery added quality coffee to its offering in the summer of 2015, opening a cafe space in the open-plan bakery, so it now serves huevos rancheros baked eggs and stacks of french toast laden with maple syrup, spiced apple, toasted pecans and bacon, alongside an ever expanding patisserie counter menu.

Whether you're after a relaxed sit-in brunch under the hanging cacti in the conservatory, or a pain au chocolat and a loaf to take home and eat in bed, this is a must-visit.

INSIDER'S TIP LOOK OUT FOR THE BREAD MAKING CLASSES, POP UP BRUNCH CLUBS AND PIZZA NIGHTS

Everything's made from scratch on site, including the jam on the toast, granola and the giant marshmallow floating on top of the Valrhona hot chocolate.

Workshop's Cult of Done espresso is handled with professional care, so the coffee's as good as the cakes. Which means, of course, that you'll want to visit all the time – for a "coffee".

KEY ROASTER
Workshop

BREWING METHODS
Espresso,
AeroPress

MACHINE
La Marzocco
Linea 2

GRINDERS
Mahlkonig EK43
Anfim Super
Caimano

OPENING HOURS
Tue-Sat 9am-6pm
Sun 9am-3pm

 Gluten FREE

 COFFEE BEANS AVAILABLE

 SOYA MILK AVAILABLE

 CYCLE FRIENDLY

 OUTDOOR SEATING

 FAMILY FRIENDLY

 DISABLED ACCESS

www.forgebakehouse.co.uk   T: 01142 588987

f Forge Bakehouse   🐦 @forgebakehouse   📷 @forgebakehouse

№70. STOKES COLLECTION CAFE

Danes Terrace, Lincoln, Lincolnshire, LN2 1LP.

Housed within the Collection Museum, a stone's throw from the Usher Gallery and beautiful Temple Gardens, Lincoln's Stokes Collection Cafe offers museum visitors (or sneaky souls who just want to make a beeline for the cakes) a haven for quality coffee and food.

Choose from the signature collection of blended speciality teas or freshly roasted coffees, or enjoy an encounter of the speciality coffee kind with something from the brew bar such as Jamaican Blue Mountain, Ethiopian Hunda Oli or the Nicaraguan Santa Maria (exclusive to Stokes).

INSIDER'S TIP VISIT FOR THE WEEKLY SUNDAY BRUNCH WITH LIVE MUSIC

When it comes to accompaniments, we'd plump for the butterscotch waffles anytime, but you'll also find generously filled sandwiches, eggs benedict and freshly-made crêpes on the locally-sourced, homemade menu. If you've got kids in tow, you can relax in the knowledge that they're well catered for, as are gluten-dodgers.

Inside, the space is stylish and comfortable while in warmer weather a large sunny terrace (where furry visitors are welcome too) is the place to head.

KEY ROASTER
Stokes Coffee

BREWING METHODS
Espresso, filter, AeroPress, V60

MACHINES
Sanremo, Bravilor

GRINDER
Mahlkonig

OPENING HOURS
Mon-Sun
10am-4pm

www.stokes-coffee.co.uk   T: 01522 523548

Stokes Coffee   @stokescoffee   @stokescoffee

№71. COFFEE AROMA

24 Guildhall Street, Lincoln, Lincolnshire, LN1 1TR.

The choice of areas in which to enjoy a coffee makes Lincoln's Coffee Aroma hugely appealing. And it's easy to hang around for a long time at this three storey 18th century building in the city's historic centre – in fact, that's what its current owner, Andrew Carnell, did before he eventually bought the coffee shop.

The self confessed coffee fanatic knows the worth of finding that perfect place to catch up on work, or your social media feed, while enjoying a good brew. His instincts were right too – since taking over the turnover has doubled.

INSIDER'S TIP NEW THIS YEAR IS A PERFECTED COLD BREW

There's a busy communal bar downstairs – with outdoor seating – a first floor drawing room and a cosy snug with sofas and books. And right at the top of the building is the pleasant surprise of a gloriously sunny attic space.

A cafe with soul, Coffee Aroma has a loyal following, a range of wines, continental beers and cocktails, and a constant line-up of live music and comedy nights.

KEY ROASTER
Has Bean

BREWING METHODS
Espresso, Chemex, Kalita Wave, Hario cold brew, AeroPress

MACHINE
La Spaziale S5EK Group 2

GRINDERS
Mahlkonig K30 Vario, Tanzania

OPENING HOURS
Mon-Thurs
8am-7pm
Fri-Sat
8am-11pm
Sun 10am-5pm

www.coffeearoma.co.uk   T: 01522 569892

f Coffee Aroma   @coffee_aroma   @aromacoffeehouse

№72. STOKES HIGH BRIDGE CAFE

207-209 High Street, Lincoln, Lincolnshire, LN5 7AU.

A Lincoln institute, the Stokes High Bridge Cafe offers all the quaint charm you'd expect from a historic Tudor building with waiting staff in period dress – but without a cup of stewed tea or curly sandwich in sight.

Instead, Stokes offers a splendid coffee selection of single origin beans and blends such as Old Brown Java and Kenyan Gatomboyan alongside its own blends, including a Blue Mountain blend, a breakfast blend and the robust Full of Beans blend. Alternatively, you can take a trip to the Brew Bar for something a little more unusual.

INSIDER'S TIP
TEA-LOVERS SHOULD TRY "FLO'S MIX" INVENTED IN THE 1970S BY ONE OF STOKES' LONG-SERVING WAITRESSES

True to its roots, the Stokes High Bridge Cafe also boasts more than 30 loose leaf teas, including some award-winning, house blends.

With hearty breakfasts, lunches and treat-yourself afternoon teas, the menu centres around a wide selection of homemade dishes, created with locally-sourced ingredients, wherever possible.

KEY ROASTER
Stokes Coffee

BREWING METHODS
Espresso, filter, AeroPress, V60

MACHINES
Sanremo, Bravilor

GRINDER
Mahlkonig

OPENING HOURS
Mon-Sat 8am-5pm
Sun 11.30am-4pm

 Gluten FREE

 COFFEE BEANS AVAILABLE

 SOYA MILK AVAILABLE

 WIFI

 OUTDOOR SEATING

 COFFEE COURSES AVAILABLE

 FAMILY FRIENDLY

 DISABLED ACCESS

www.stokes-coffee.co.uk   T: 01522 523548

f Stokes Coffee   🐦 @stokescoffee   📷 @stokescoffee

SALTED
CHOCOLATE
COOKIES

SALTED
CHOCOLATE
COOKIES

SOUR CHERRY
AND ANISEED
COOKIES

SOUR CHERRY
AND ANISEED
COOKIES

BANANA BREAD
GRANOLA

BANANA B
GRANO

Hazelnut
praline

Rhubarb
curd

£2 out
£2·40 IN

Lemon fool

Coriander hummus,
chargrilled peppers, tomato
& spinach leaves

£3.80

MORE GOOD
CUPS

So many cool places to drink coffee ...

73.

1901 CAFFE BISTRO

St George's Terrace, Jesmond,
Newcastle upon Tyne, NE2 2DL.

T: 01913 409774

f 1901 Caffe Bistro
w @1901cafe
@ @cafe1901jesmond

74.

BUNKER COFFEE & KITCHEN

9-11 Carliol Square,
Newcastle upon Tyne, NE1 6UF.

www.bunkercoffee.co.uk

f Bunker Coffee and Kitchen
w @bunkercoffeencl
@ @bunker_ncl

75.

PINK LANE COFFEE

1 Pink Lane, Newcastle upon Tyne,
NE1 5DW.

www.pinklanecoffee.co.uk

f Pink Lane Coffee
w @pinklanecoffee
@ @pinklanecoffee

76.

ARCH SIXTEEN CAFE

Arch 16, High Level Parade, Wellington
Street, Gateshead, NE8 2AJ.

T: 01914 900208

f Arch Sixteen Café
w @archsixteen
@ @archsixteencafe

77.

FLAT WHITE CAFE

21a Elvet Bridge, Durham, DH1 3AA.

www.flatwhitedurham.co.uk

T: 07936 449291

f Flat White Cafe
w @flatwhitedurham
@ @flatwhitedurham

78.

THE WOLFHOUSE KITCHEN

Lindeth Road, Silverdale, Carnforth,
Lancashire, LA5 0TX.

T: 01524 702024

f The Wolfhouse Kitchen
w @wolfhousewolf
@ @wolfhousekitchen

79.

EXCHANGE COFFEE COMPANY – BLACKBURN MARKET

Stall F9, Blackburn Market,
Church Street, Lancashire, BB1 5AF.

www.exchangecoffee.co.uk

T: 01254 669195

w @exchange_coffee
@ @exchange_coffee

80.
ROAST COFFEE & KITCHEN
33 Crosby Road North, Liverpool,
L22 4QB.

T: 01515 381820

f Roast Coffee & Kitchen
y @roastcoffeeshop
@roast_coffeeandkitchend

81.
COFFEE & FANDISHA
5 Brick Street, Liverpool, L1 0BL.

T: 01517 086492

f Coffee & Fandisha
y @coffeefandisha
@coffeeandfandisha

82.
THE BARISTA'S COFFEE CO.
9 Watergate Street, Chester, Cheshire,
CH1 2LB.

www.thebaristas.co.uk

T: 01244 400045

f The Barista's
y @Thebaristasches
@thebaristaschester

83.
NORTH TEA POWER
36 Tib Street, Manchester, M4 1LA.

www.northteapower.co.uk

T: 01618 333073

f North Tea Power
y @northteapower
@northteapower

84.
FOUNDATION COFFEE HOUSE
Sevendale House, Lever Street,
Manchester, M1 1JB.

www.foundationcoffeehouse.co.uk

T: 01612 388633

f Foundation Coffee House
y @fdncoffee
@fdncoffee

85.
EZRA & GIL
20 Hilton Street, Manchester,
Northern Quarter, M1 1FR.

www.ezraandgil.co.uk

y @ezra_gil
@ezraandgil

86.
IDLE HANDS
8a Gateway House, Station Approach,
Piccadilly, Manchester, M1 2GH.

www.idlehandscoffee.com

y @idlehandscoffee
@idlehandscoffee

87.
MANCOCO
Arch 84, Hewitt Street, Manchester,
M15 4GB.

www.mancoco.co.uk

T: 01612 371916

f ManCoCo
y @mancocoltd
@mancocoltd

88.

THE ANCHOR COFFEE HOUSE

508 Moss Lane East, Manchester,
M14 4PA.

www.anchorcoffee.co.uk

T: 01612 488772

f The Anchor Coffee House
@anchorcoffee
@anchorcoffee

89.

TEA HIVE

53 Manchester Road, Chorlton,
Manchester, M21 9PW.

www.teahive.co.uk

T: 01618 810569

f Tea Hive
@teahivetweets
@teahivechorlton

90.

TANDEM COFFEE HOUSE

47 Lower Hillgate, Stockport, SK1 1JQ.

www.tandemcoffeehouse.co.uk

T: 07542 866349

f Tandem Coffee House
@tandemcoffeesk1
@tandem_coffee

91.

THE PERKY PEACOCK

Lendal Bridge, York, YO1 7DJ.

www.perkypeacockcoffee.co.uk

f theperkypeacocklendal
@theperkypeacock

92.

STANLEY & RAMONA

30a Bishopthorpe Road, York, YO23 1JJ.

www.stanleyandramona.co.uk

T: 01904 659166

f Stanley & Ramona
@stanandramona
@stanleyandramona

93.

EXCHANGE COFFEE COMPANY – SKIPTON

10 Gargrave Road, Skipton,
North Yorkshire, BD23 1PJ.

www.exchangecoffee.co.uk

T: 01756 795649

@exchange_coffee
@exchange_coffee

94.

EXCHANGE COFFEE COMPANY – TODMORDEN

Todmorden Market Hall, Brook Street,
Todmorden, OL14 5AJ.

www.exchangecoffee.co.uk

T: 01706 83993

@exchange_coffee
@exchange_coffee

95.

EMILY'S BY DE LUCA BOUTIQUE

The Brontë Birthplace, 72-74 Market
Street, Thornton, Bradford, BD13 3HF.

www.delucaboutique.co.uk

T: 01274 834853

f Emily's by De Luca Boutique - The Brontë Birthplace
w @emilys_bronte
@ @emilysbydelucaboutique

96.

SOCIABLE FOLK

10 Wellington Place, Leeds, LS1 4AP.

www.sociablefolk.co.uk

T: 01132 431840

f Sociable Folk
w @sociablefolk
@ @sociable_folk

97.

LA BOTTEGA MILANESE - THE LIGHT

The Headrow, Leeds, West Yorkshire,
LS1 8TL.

www.labottegamilanese.co.uk

T: 01132 454242

f La Bottega Milanese
w @bottegamilanese
@ @labottegamilanese

98.

MRS ATHA'S

Central Road, Leeds, LS1 6DE.

www.mrsathasleeds.com

f Mrs Atha's
w @mrsathasleeds
@ @mrsathas

99.

CIELO - CROSSGATES

Unit 13, Crossgates Shopping Centre,
Leeds, LS11 8ET.

www.cielouk.com

f Cielo Coffee
w @cielouk
@ @cielocoffee

100.

CIELO - EXPRESS BAR

Garforth Library, 1-5 Main St, Garforth,
Leeds, LS25 1DU.

www.cielouk.com

f Cielo Coffee
w @cielouk
@ @cielocoffee

101.

STEAM YARD COFFEE CO.

Unit 1-2 Aberdeen Court,
97 Division Street, Sheffield, S1 4GE.

f Steam Yard
w @steamyard
@ @steamyard

102.

BRAGAZZIS

224-226 Abbeydale Road, Sheffield,
S7 1FL.

www.bragazzis.co.uk

T: 01142 5801483

f Bragazzis
@ @bragazzis

ROASTERS

103. LUCKIE BEANS

3 Love Lane, Berwick upon Tweed, Northumberland, TD15 1AR.
www.luckiebeans.co.uk   T: 07810 446537

f Luckie Beans   🐦 @luckiebeans   📷 @luckie_beans

Luckie Beans may be one of northern England's newest speciality roasters, but a passion for the dark stuff has been a long-term love affair for owner Jamie McLuckie.

'A NATURAL AT THE ART OF ROASTING, JAMIE SCOOPED FIFTH PLACE AT THE UK'S FIRST ROASTING CHAMPIONSHIPS'

Drinking coffee since the age of three (yep, really), Jamie's interest in a quality cup flourished while he toured the world working in the music industry. '*I visited some amazing coffee shops while travelling with my job*,' he explains, '*so I witnessed how different cultures use coffee in different ways.*' And in 2015, when his wife fell pregnant, the opportunity arose to turn his passion into a career.

A natural at the art of roasting, Jamie scooped fifth place at the UK's first Roasting Championships the very same year, with a meticulous philosophy that saw him pip to the post the very roasters that inspired him to launch Luckie Beans.

'*We're not churning out coffee for the sake of it*,' says Jamie, '*we take time to make the coffee the best it can be.*'

You'll find the house blend Love Lane (named after the street that England's most northerly roaster calls home) at restaurants and bistros across the country, and if you want to strike it luckie at home, beans are available as one-off orders or monthly subscriptions.

Make sure to explore the range of single origins such as the Malawi AAA with its moreish maple, date and kumquat flavours.

ᴹᴬᴾᴺᵒ104. TYNEMOUTH COFFEE COMPANY

Unit 4, Back Stormont Street, North Shields, Tyne and Wear, NE29 0EY.
www.tynemouthcoffee.com T: 01912 600995

f Tynemouth Coffee Company 🐦 @tynemouthcoffee 📷 @tynemouth_coffee

They may only have been roasting for a few months, but the team of six behind Tynemouth certainly knows more than a thing or two about coffee. *'We've been going since 2009, but mainly in the machine and equipment side of things,'* says Paul Thompson, a co-director along with Stuart Douglas.

Having built up an enviable reputation for knowing everything there is to know about coffee machines and barista training, and after working with a specialist roaster for 10 years, Paul and Stuart are now applying the same level of meticulous knowledge to their own coffees. And let's face it - who better to start experimenting with roasting complexities than a team of coffee engineering geeks?

'WHO BETTER TO START EXPERIMENTING WITH ROASTING COMPLEXITIES THAN A TEAM OF COFFEE ENGINEERING GEEKS?'

Paul modestly confesses that after 25 years in coffee (working as a barista, then with the machine sales and training) he *'knows a bit about it and how it works. And we are all good at the technical geeky part,'* he adds.

Tynemouth produces artisan, small batch coffee for both wholesale and online sales and you'll find them at food festivals across the North East and beyond. Every batch that goes out the door is sampled for consistency and Paul says their coffees are continuously evolving. *'We're always looking for perfection,'* he says. *'With one blend, we're on our eighth version of it, and it's not finished yet. Each version has been great,'* he explains, *'but there's always another way you can do it.'*

And of course they still stock, install and service both commercial and domestic espresso machines. *'If you're looking for advice on equipment for your new venture, or just looking to upgrade from your french press, give us a call,'* says Paul.

COFFEE BEANS AVAILABLE
SOLD ON SITE & ONLINE

COFFEE COURSES AVAILABLE

№105. OUSEBURN COFFEE CO.

Foundry Lane Studios, Foundry Lane, Newcastle, Tyne and Wear, NE6 1LH.
www.ouseburncoffee.co.uk T: 07572 138729

f Ouseburn Coffee Co 🐦 @ouseburncoffee 📷 @ouseburncoffee

OCC is an independent roastery at the forefront of the speciality coffee scene in the North East.

Launched in 2012, the business is dedicated to offering a highly selective range of the finest seasonal crops, roasted in small batches to ensure consistent quality.

'AS NEWCASTLE'S FIRST INDIE ROASTERY, IT CONTINUES TO INNOVATE'

A few years on and things have really taken off for this coffee crew, who have gone from selling their coffee at local markets (which they still do) to launching their own cafe, Harvest in Jesmond, as well as a new outpost at the rather glam Fenwick Food Hall in the city.

As Newcastle's first indie roastery, it continues to innovate, setting the benchmark for quality: all the beans are ethically sourced, speciality grade and roasted at Foundry Lane to be bagged up on the same day.

In addition to supplying trade customers and coffee enthusiasts, home brewers can visit Foundry Lane between 9am-5pm on weekdays to buy fresh beans, talk to the guys or just enjoy a cup of freshly roasted coffee.

As well as its flagship espresso blend and range of speciality coffee, OCC offers regular micro-lots and bi-monthly seasonal specials following the global coffee harvests. This way the customer can enjoy the finest crops while learning more about the coffee landscape.

And to top it all, OCC is working towards becoming the UK's first carbon neutral company. Hats off.

COFFEE BEANS AVAILABLE
SOLD ON SITE & ONLINE

COFFEE COURSES AVAILABLE

☛106. CARVETII COFFEE

The Roastery, Embleton, Cockermouth, Cumbria, CA13 9YA.

www.carvetiicoffee.co.uk   T: 01768 776979

f Carvetii Coffee 🐦 @carvetiicoffee ⬚ @carvetiicoffee

After initially helping to set up a coffee shop in north Wales back in 2006, Angharad Macdonald and Gareth Kemble turned their attentions to roasting.

They were on a mission to discover and create coffees which were not only extremely high quality, but also ethically and sustainably sourced.

'A CRAFT THAT BEGAN WITH EXPERIMENTS IN THE KITCHEN FRYING PAN'

Angharad's roasting ability (a craft developed over many years, beginning with experiments in the kitchen frying pan) and Gareth's almost fanatical interest in research and keeping up with the latest global coffee developments, made them a winning team.

So Carvetii's coffee is very carefully sourced – they know the origin of everything they buy, often down to the farm where it was grown – and beans are selected according to the season (and never air freighted). This year they're also launching some limited edition coffees from very small lots which will only be around for a short time.

'All our coffee is sold as whole bean,' says Gareth. *'It's a principle we firmly believe offers the best quality to our customers, and we've adhered to it since we opened our doors in 2011.'*

Always keen to share their knowledge, they've continued to develop the training and education side of the business, dedicating much of their time to helping others through training, workshops and demos.

Although the roastery isn't open to the public, watch out for occasional special events – or sign up for a brewing or espresso course.

№107. RED BANK COFFEE ROASTERS

Unit 4b, Lake Road Estate, Coniston, Cumbria, LA21 8EW.

redbankroasters.com T: 01539 449185

f Red Bank Coffee Roasters 🐦 @redbankroasters 📷 @redbankroasters

L aunched just over a year ago with the mission to show Cumbria just how good coffee can be, Red Bank Coffee Roasters has had a remarkable start – with its coffee now being offered in many of the Lake District's best cafes, delis and restaurants.

'WITH BIODEGRADABLE PACKAGING, RED BANK'S COFFEE IS AS EASY ON THE CONSCIENCE AS IT IS ON THE PALATE'

Founded by Tom Prestwich, and ably assisted by recent recruit Chris, Red Bank's ethically-sourced coffee is hand roasted in small batches to ensure freshness. The line-up changes regularly too, so they are always offering coffee that's seasonal and great tasting.

'It can be hard to persuade people to take that first step to better quality coffee,' says Tom, *'but for those who have, the idea of going back is unthinkable.'*

In addition to its single origins, Red Bank has recently launched two seasonal blends: Penny Rock which delivers beautiful caramel sweetness, and Deer Bolt which offers, *'more of a kick up the hind'*.

And with biodegradable packaging decorated with local artwork, Red Bank's coffee is as easy on the eye and conscience as it is on the palate. *'We work in one of the most beautiful places on the planet and want to help keep it that way,'* smiles Tom.

COFFEE BEANS AVAILABLE
SOLD ON SITE
& ONLINE

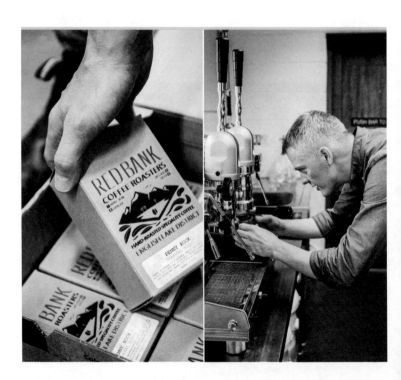

108. FARRER'S

9 Shap Road Industrial Estate, Kendal, Cumbria, LA9 6NZ.
www.farrerscoffee.co.uk T: 01539 720020

f Farrers 🐦 @farrers_coffee

It's been a notable year for this roastery, which is saying something when you consider the business can trace its roots back to 1819.

The tea and coffee merchant, founded by John Farrer in Kendal all those years ago, has been with its current owners since the 1980s. Still a family business, it has a coffee ancestry going back two generations and a team which includes employees with more than 20 years' roasting experience. That knowledge will be put to good use this year with its super new training centre – part of a two year project to redevelop the Farrer's site, which includes the roastery and machine service workshops.

'We've always offered training,' says managing director Simon Walsh, *'but it was usually at customers' premises, which isn't always ideal. And as a satellite of the Beverage Standards Association, we can now offer City and Guilds Level 2 barista training.'*

The spacious and high tech facility has wow factor in abundance and is an equal match to the coffee being roasted next door.

Beans come from a wide range of sources, including new micro-lots, as well as farmers with whom Farrer's has relationships going back more than half a century.

Three roasters, ranging from a 1.5kg to 60kg, mean the team can create a variety of profiles, and prides itself on crafting small batches which can then be accurately recreated on a larger scale.

'THE BUSINESS CAN TRACE ITS ROOTS BACK TO 1819'

Another new offering – for both trade and home customers – is the quarterly seasonal selection. These speciality coffees are created from small batches and are only available for a limited time, providing an extra dimension to Farrer's line-up of over 50 different coffees.

6 MODULES,
3 LEVELS,
1 DIPLOMA

Get your coffee diploma with **SCAE** and further your career.

Learn more about the world's most comprehensive
coffee education on **scae.com**
or call +44 (0) 1245 426060 for further details.

MAP No. 109. RINALDO'S SPECIALITY COFFEE & TEA

Unit 20, Summerlands Trading Estate, Endmoor, Cumbria, LA8 0FB.

www.rinscoffee.com   T: 07947 093226

f Rinaldo's Speciality Coffee & Tea   🐦 @rinscoffee   ✉ @rinscoffee

COFFEE BEANS AVAILABLE SOLD ON SITE & ONLINE

COFFEE COURSES AVAILABLE

Rinaldo's must be a contender for the most heartwarming coffee story in this year's guide; how many can say they bought their first roaster with the help of 140 members of the public?

The crowdfunding approach clearly worked for Rinaldo Colombi and proved that good things do come to those who wait – and work hard.

'I WOKE UP ONE MORNING AND THOUGHT, "GOD! I'VE BOUGHT A COFFEE VAN"'

Born in Cumbria to Italian parents, Rin grew up with a passion for good food and drink. *'Mum and dad got us into stove tops from an early age. I took my six cup stove top to university when I went to do a design degree, and used to down it in one go,'* he laughs, *'I thought that was normal!'*

Clearly, coffee was destined to play a big part in his life, and after 15 years in the corporate world, he took the plunge.

'I woke up one morning and thought, "God! I've bought a coffee van." I left my job and six weeks later I was up and running. It felt so right though; I'd wanted to work for myself for years.'

After taking his van around the shows, weddings and cycle sportives of Cumbria, introducing people to the world of high level coffee and latte art, it was a natural progression to start roasting – with the financial help of many of his happy customers who gave their pledges in return for a free cup or two.

Rin's just as keen on speciality tea and he's even turned his hand to making bespoke barista aprons – so that design degree came in useful after all.

№110. J. ATKINSON & CO.

12 China Street, Lancaster, Lancashire, LA1 1EX.
www.thecoffeehopper.com T: 01524 65470

f The Shop - J.Atkinson & Co. 🐦 @coffeehopper 📷 @coffeehopper

A tkinson's has been a fervently independent, caffeine-fuelled, family-run firm since 1837.

It was re-launched in 2005 by the Steel family and so, although the place is steeped in tea and coffee history, it now pioneers new boundaries in its search for, 'the sweet spot of the bean' as described by master roaster Ian Steel.

A significant operation, it supplies coffee and tea to the people of north Lancashire and way beyond, through its roastery and shop in the centre of Lancaster.

'A CLASH OF HERITAGE AND INNOVATION'

There's always a pleasing mix of old and new, such as recent plans to create a brand new roastery on site – which is due to open as we go to print.

'It's space age meets steam age,' says a delighted Ian. 'We'll have a state-of-the-art shiny stainless steel Loring Smart Roast sitting alongside the black cast iron 1930s open-flame Whitmees, in a clash of heritage and innovation.'

J. Atkinson and Co. continues to work with small family farms whenever it can, sourcing from a wealth of countries, including El Salvador, Honduras, Guatemala, Costa Rica, Cuba, Colombia, Brazil, Peru, Ethiopia, Kenya, Rwanda, India and Indonesia.

'We know most of the farmers we now source from,' says Ian, 'and we aim to stick with them. So we'll commit to forward contracts, sometimes agreeing to buy coffee which is still on the bush. Of course this guarantees greater financial security for them and some great exclusive coffees for us.'

Atkinson's is undeniably a destination venue for coffee fans with its shop, The Hall cafe and now, sandwiched between, its new roastery. Meet you there for a coffee.

COFFEE BEANS AVAILABLE
SOLD ON SITE & ONLINE

COFFEE COURSES AVAILABLE

MAP № 111. EXCHANGE COFFEE COMPANY

The Old Chapel Roastery, Islington, Canterbury Street, Blackburn, Lancashire, BB2 2HP.
www.exchangecoffee.co.uk T: 01254 665663 / 01200 442270

f Exchange Coffee Company 🐦 @exchange_coffee ☒ @exchange_coffee

The team leading the operation at Exchange Coffee Company shares an incredible 135 years roasting experience between them, so no wonder it enjoys a position as one of the North's most prestigious speciality coffee empires, with a whopping 32 Great Taste Awards.

If it's riding high now, the beginnings were much more humble, with owner Mark Smith roasting beans in his garden shed 30 years ago.

'ONE OF THE NORTH'S MOST PRESTIGIOUS SPECIALITY COFFEE EMPIRES, WITH A WHOPPING 32 GREAT TASTE AWARDS'

To date, Exchange has three roasting shops, in Clitheroe, Blackburn and Skipton, two coffee bars in Blackburn and Todmorden markets and two coffee vans. There's also a thriving wholesale coffee roastery which is housed in a converted 1764 Baptist chapel in Blackburn, where a 1978 Probat GN25 roaster sits at the heart of the operation.

Mark has always been particular about the terroir of his coffee, knowing that geography, climate and geology have a huge impact on the profile and quality of the beans, and his team works closely with green coffee importers to source single estate, Rainforest Alliance and micro-lot coffees. *'It means we are able to select some amazing coffees of differing varietals, processing and terroir,'* he says.

Working alongside Cimbali and Expobar, Exchange is well versed in offering advice to start-up coffee ventures and offers barista training and service back-up. But it's when Mark and his roasting team - Richard, Chris, Jo, Nathan, Lucie and Adam – start talking coffee that the excitement and sense of adventure really shines through, with a passion for coffee as strong as the day Exchange started all those years ago.

COFFEE BEANS AVAILABLE SOLD ON SITE & ONLINE

COFFEE COURSES AVAILABLE

MAP N° 112. ROBERTS & CO.

The Coffee Roastery, Cedar Farm, Back Lane, Mawdesley, Ormskirk, Lancashire, L40 3SY.
www.e-coffee.co.uk   T: 01704 822433

f Roberts & Co Roastery

Roasters of the finest coffee beans from around the world, Roberts and Co. uses vintage Whitmee roasters to create single origin coffees and bespoke blends for baristas to turn into exceptional espresso and fantastic filter coffee.

Established in Liverpool in 1891, it's still run by the same family, although they're now based at Cedar Farm in Mawdesley which was originally a working pig farm.

Tea is where it all started for Roberts and Co. - they didn't start roasting coffee until the 1930s, but they now concentrate on speciality coffee, along with selling a range of quality teas and equipment.

While much of the business is about supplying coffee wholesale, brew geeks can rock up to the farm to buy beans and get a quick hit at the busy espresso bar within the roastery. There's also a cafe,

which is mostly vegetarian and specialises in sourcing locally, so you can fuel up and feel good at the same time.

Most people love the Espresso Napoli blend, which is the most popular in the range.

'BREW GEEKS CAN ROCK UP TO THE FARM TO BUY BEANS AND GET A QUICK HIT AT THE ESPRESSO BAR'

'It's important to us to source and roast the finest single origin and estate coffees. We also blend different coffees to suit different methods of coffee making,' says John, the fourth generation co-owner of the company, along with his daughter Amy. 'To us, coffee is like wine, with a great variety of flavours to enjoy.'

113. CROSBY COFFEE

Unit 14, Bridge Road Industrial Estate, Litherland, Liverpool, Merseyside, L21 2QG.
www.crosbycoffee.co.uk   T: 01515 385454

f Crosby Coffee   ⌨ @coffeecrosby   📷 @crosbycoffeeltd

COFFEE
BEANS
AVAILABLE
SOLD ON SITE
& ONLINE

☕ COFFEE
COURSES
AVAILABLE

W hen Crosby Coffee's Jack Foster started roasting coffee on a tiny roaster in his mum's front room, he had no idea it would spiral into a thriving business as one of Liverpool's original, homegrown roasteries.

It all took off when Jack bagged up some of his coffee to sell to locals at foodie markets in Crosby and Waterloo. The response from customers was astonishing, and Jack was selling out each week, as well as getting phone calls from customers trying to track down more.

'THE RESPONSE WAS ASTONISHING, WITH JACK SELLING OUT EACH WEEK'

Realising he was on to something, Jack kept going, and within 18 months had moved out of the front room and into a unit at a nearby precinct – with a bigger 1kg roaster to play on.

That was in November 2015, and he's already looking at upgrading the roaster to a 10kg, as demand is again outstripping supply.

Crosby Coffee's success seems to come from three sources. Firstly, the quality of the coffee, which takes the shape of seven or eight single origins and three blends, including the seasonal espresso blend, the lighter Trio blend and Iron Men.

Secondly, Jack's background in catering has given him a thorough understanding of what the hospitality industry requires, and thirdly, the loyalty of the good people of Liverpool to a local company that's itself supporting local businesses.

It's a winning combination, and one that's recently earned Crosby Coffee a contract to supply coffee to some of the VIP areas at Aintree Racecourse for the Grand National.

Visit the takeout brew bar on site where all the beans can be purchased from Tuesday to Saturday.

114. JOE BLACK COFFEE

Unit 30, Millers Bridge Industrial Estate, Seymour Street, Liverpool, Merseyside, L20 1EE.
www.joeblackcoffee.co.uk   T: 07770 928652

f Joe Black Coffee   🐦 @joeblackcoffee   📷 @joeblackcoffeeuk

If you're looking for a coffee company that'll not only roast your coffee but also supply equipment, syrups, sugar, barista training, machine servicing, coffee branding, teas and soft drinks, then Joe Black's your man.

The team has been roasting coffee on Merseyside for more than sixty years (it was very possibly Joe Black coffee that The Beatles sipped as they sat in those 1960s coffee shops). And now it even provides custom packaging, labelling and dispatching of coffee and accompaniments.

'IT EVEN PROVIDES CUSTOM PACKAGING AND LABELLING OF COFFEE'

The team still uses traditional flame-roasted production techniques, roasting on Probat roasters, and supplies fresh beans to some of the North West's top restaurants and upcoming coffee shops.

With a decent sized collection of coffees, it meets the needs of a wide range of industry customers, including providing a new selection of artisan blends along with a speciality range from different bean growing regions of the globe.

Home brewers can also buy direct from the website to get coffee delivered to their door.

COFFEE BEANS AVAILABLE
SOLD ON SITE & ONLINE

COFFEE COURSES AVAILABLE

≡115. NEIGHBOURHOOD COFFEE

Unit 89, Chadwick Court Industrial Centre, Chadwick Street, Liverpool, Merseyside, L3 7EY.
www.neighbourhoodcoffee.co.uk   T: 01512 366741

f Neighbourhood Coffee   🐦 @nhoodcoffee   ☑ @neighbourhoodcoffee

The foundation of the Neighbourhood story lies in owners Ed and Chris' history as coffee traders for Schluter in Liverpool.

Experienced at sourcing and buying green beans (Ed even lived in Ethiopia for a while), it was a natural move to set up on their own, eventually.

'SELF CONFESSED TRADERS AT HEART, CHRIS AND ED HAVE CUPPED THOUSANDS OF COFFEES IN THE LAST EIGHT YEARS'

And the result? A rapidly growing roasting company that's discovering exceptional beans from across the world – and not just their former stomping ground of Africa.

Recently the chaps have been revved up about a Colombian coffee which was placed 12th of 500 lots in the Cauca Best Cup, as well as excited about a new direct trade with Brazil, as they're increasingly aiming to buy direct from farmers. *'We want to build relationships and return year after year, to help the farmers we are buying from,'* says Ed.

Indeed, they sent a lot of the profits from their first year in business to help build a nursery and school in Tanzania.

Self confessed traders at heart, Chris and Ed see their advantage in having cupped thousands of coffees in the last eight years, *'so we know what's good value and what's hype'*, and that confidence has led the pair to boldly invest in a chunky 15kg Giesen roaster and proper premises for this first incarnation of their vision. That means they've the capacity to train customers in-house and reach their goal of doubling their 200kg weekly output in a year's time. Will they do it? You betcha.

№116. ADAMS + RUSSELL COFFEE ROASTERS

8 Appin Road, Argyle Industrial Estate, Birkenhead, CH41 9HH.
www.adamsandrussell.co.uk T: 01516 474210

f Adams & Russell Fresh Coffee 🐦 @adamsandrussell 📷 @adamsandrussell

It's not often you find a roastery that produces 30 different single origin coffees, so one which produces speciality coffee with the pedigree that Adams and Russell can claim is a rarity.

Set up by two coffee pioneers in 1978, Adams and Russell began supplying quality coffee to local cafes and restaurants in Liverpool and on the Wirral: 'we were roasting coffee before it became cool,' says Tristan Bartlett.

'THE BIG THING THAT'S CHANGED IS THE AVAILABILITY AND QUALITY OF SINGLE PLANTATION COFFEE'

And it's testament to its founding principles that not much has changed since those early days. The team, now made up of eight barista-trained coffee enthusiasts, still uses traditional gas flamed 15kg roasters to produce their exceptional coffee.

'The big thing that's different,' according to Tristan, 'is the availability and quality of single plantation coffee. We have sourced beans from farms in Cape Verde, Nepal and Guatemala which are outstanding. A lot of education and time has gone into local economies and it shows in the coffee.'

Roasting in small batches also means they can create very individual bespoke blends and ensures freshly roasted coffee in every bag.

As a member of the Fairtrade Association and Rainforest Alliance, Adams and Russell always aims to source ethically produced coffee, and with a growing coffee school affiliated with SCAE up and running, the Birkenhead roastery is certainly one to watch on the coffee circuit.

COFFEE BEANS AVAILABLE
SOLD ON SITE & ONLINE

COFFEE COURSES AVAILABLE

MAP № 117. HEART AND GRAFT COFFEE ROASTERY

Artwork Atelier, 95 Greengate, Salford, Greater Manchester, M3 7NG.

www.heartandgraft.co.uk T: 07743 895763

🐦 @heartandgraft 📷 heartandgraft

'It's been a mental year', says James Guard of Manchester's Heart and Graft Coffee Roastery.

'We're seeing the cafes we supply go from strength to strength, and a surge in all sorts of businesses wanting to improve the quality of the coffee they serve.'

"WE'RE INCREDIBLY EXCITED ABOUT BRINGING A LITTLE COFFEE GEM WE'VE DISCOVERED TO MANCHESTER"

It's good news for James and his colleague Sean as it means that in addition to sourcing speciality coffee from single farms, estates and co-ops around the world, they've been able to make their first foray into directly traded coffee: 'we're incredibly excited about bringing a little coffee gem we've discovered to Manchester,' he smiles.

'Everything is bought and roasted on the basis of flavour, and we blind cup it all. We're developing a roast style that we're really happy with and are always looking to draw out as much sweetness as possible from a coffee, so it can accentuate the delicate fruit flavours and reveal all its beautiful potential.'

The regular range now numbers six coffees, from Barnraiser, its well known chocolate and caramel espresso, to Loveshack, the sweet, juicy and full bodied Central or South American blend.

'The specific coffees we use change seasonally, of course,' says James, 'but these coffee archetypes help people identify a profile they know they'll enjoy.'

118. ANCOATS COFFEE CO.

Unit 9, Royal Mills, 17 Redhill Street, Ancoats, Manchester, M4 5BA.
www.ancoats-coffee.co.uk   T: 01612 283211

f Ancoats Coffee Co.   🐦 @ancoatscoffee   📷 @ancoatscoffeeco

From the Industrial revolution to the coffee revolution, the Ancoats area of Manchester has played its part.

Named after this gritty, working part of the city, Ancoats Coffee Co. has gone back to the roots of the revolution and has recently moved from a basic unit into the completely renovated, Grade II-listed Royal Mills development, which was the site of one of the first cotton mills in England.

'FACTORY FEATURES ARE ALL PART OF THE CHARM - STEEL COLUMNS AND BARE BRICK WALLS PROVIDING AN URBAN VIBE'

The Giesen roaster sits in the middle of Ancoats' contemporary cafe, and the mill features are all part of the charm - steel columns, bare brick walls and vaulted ceilings providing an urban vibe.

Owner and head roaster, Jamie Boland, cooks up green beans from all over the world. The current offering includes single origin beans from exclusive micro-lots in Nicaragua (Finca El Bosque and Samaria), Costa Rica (Finca La Plata) and Colombia (El Limbo), along with Ethiopian (Guji Liyu and Rocko Mountain Reserve), Burundi and Kenyan beans (Gakayuini PB) and those from Brazil (Rainha Da Paz).

Watching (and smelling) the beans being roasted on site takes the customers' coffee experience so much further, and you can, of course, buy the beans to take home as well as drinking coffee in a variety of styles while you're there.

COFFEE BEANS AVAILABLE
SOLD ON SITE & ONLINE

COFFEE COURSES AVAILABLE

ᴹᴬᴾ№ 119. ROUNTON COFFEE

East Rounton, Northallerton, North Yorkshire, DL6 2LG.

www.rountoncoffee.co.uk T: 07539 285197

f Rounton Coffee Roasters ✔ @rountoncoffee ✉ @rountoncoffee

Inside a handsome converted granary in the picturesque North Yorkshire village of East Rounton, you'll find the Rounton Coffee micro-roastery. With its small crew, led by founder Dave Beattie, it's dedicated to bringing speciality coffee to the people of Yorkshire - and beyond.

The award-winning team uses a 10kg capacity roaster, preparing, roasting and packing on site at The Granary. Currently supplying wholesale clients and retail customers via various outlets and food fairs, Rounton Coffee also offers a popular subscription service so coffee lovers can get freshly-roasted beans dropped conveniently through their letter box.

New this year is the opening of its cafe, called Bedford St Coffee, in the heart of Middlesbrough. It's the perfect opportunity to sample the team's roasts – you won't get fresher – as well as to indulge in a bit of speciality coffee chat – probably with one of the Daves. There are three of them: *'you have to wear a checked shirt and be called Dave to work here,'* says Dave Number One.

Especially recommended is The Granary Blend signature espresso, named after the building it's roasted in. A medium roast coffee with a smooth bodied finish, this 100 per cent speciality blend is completely traceable, sourced from certified farms, and is pretty good too.

COFFEE BEANS AVAILABLE SOLD ON SITE & ONLINE

'"YOU HAVE TO WEAR A CHECKED SHIRT AND BE CALLED DAVE TO WORK HERE," SAYS DAVE NUMBER ONE'

№120. ROOST COFFEE & ROASTERY

6 Talbot Yard, Yorkersgate, Malton, North Yorkshire, YO17 7FT.
www.roostcoffee.co.uk T: 01653 697635

f Roost Coffee 🐦 @roost_coffee 📷 @roost_coffee

Roost Coffee and Roastery is an independent, family-run business consisting of David and Ruth and their daughters Erin (a mini barista in the making) and toddler Betsy (pictured) who hangs out at the roastery each day with mum and dad.

'TODDLER BETSY HANGS OUT AT THE ROASTERY EACH DAY WITH MUM AND DAD'

Together, the crew are hand roasting in small batches from their base at the attractive Talbot Yard redevelopment in Malton.

While busy supplying speciality coffee beans to wholesale and retail customers, Roost also offers coffee fiends the opportunity to visit the roastery to try out its beans at the in-house espresso bar that's open to the public, Wednesday to Saturday from 10am-2pm. Visit to also find out more about the Rocket Espresso machines you can buy, or lease, through Roost.

It's the perfect opportunity for a bit of good in-depth coffee chat, and to find out more about the two blends that are roasted on the Diedrich IR12 roaster: Roost Espresso, a lighter, contemporary coffee and Tonto Espresso, a more traditional higher roast coffee that's named after a local Malton racehorse, Top Notch Tonto. There's a range of single origin coffees from across the globe available to taste too, as well as the Swiss Water decaf.

COFFEE BEANS AVAILABLE
SOLD ON SITE

COFFEE COURSES AVAILABLE

THE INDEPENDENT COFFEE GUIDE *Series*

KNOW WHERE'S GOOD TO GO!

AVAILABLE ONLINE NOW AT
www.indycoffee.guide

NORTHERN COFFEE GUIDE №2

SCOTTISH COFFEE GUIDE №1

SOUTH WEST COFFEE GUIDE №2

№121. YORK COFFEE EMPORIUM

Unit 5, Rose Centre, Rose Avenue, York Business Park, York, North Yorkshire, YO26 6RX.
www.yorkcoffeeemporium.co.uk   T: 01904 799399

f York Coffee Emporium   🐦 @york_coffee   ☑ @yorkcoffeeemporium

Taking on an established coffee roasting business, however small, and giving it your own personal stamp is never easy, but Laurence and Philippa Beardmore have not only achieved this feat, they've gone and done it with aplomb.

In the four years since acquiring York Coffee Emporium, they've secured its place as a high quality and award-winning roaster, producing at least 30 single origin coffees at any time.

'ANYONE FOR A WHIP MA WHOP MA GATE?'

Just a quick peek back at where it all began and Laurence's engineering credentials undoubtedly had a key part to play – he'd always loved coffee and so why not experiment with building his own roasting machines? Added to that were the visits he'd made to coffee plantations when travelling the world after his time as an Army helicopter pilot. Coffee roasting was the obvious next step.

Soon Philippa came on board too, and York Coffee Emporium started to build its reputation for skilled hand-roasting, and blending coffees from around the world.

Everything is small-batch roasted after meticulous research into roast profiles, using a choice of three roasting machines (fluid bed and drum) to optimise flavour characteristics and produce light, medium and dark roasts.

Consistency is in part due to having a Q grader in the team, and York works with small specialist importers who take care to source ethically and build relationships directly with the coffee growers.

A sense of fun comes with the quirky names for their award winning blends – anyone for a Whip Ma Whop Ma Gate? And, in addition to the coffees, it also supplies superb teas, hot chocolates and choc-coated coffee beans.

COFFEE BEANS AVAILABLE
SOLD ON SITE & ONLINE

COFFEE COURSES AVAILABLE

№122. CASA ESPRESSO

Unit 5, Briar Rhydding House, Otley Road, Shipley, Bradford, West Yorkshire, BD17 7JW.
www.casaespresso.co.uk T: 01274 595841

f Casa Espresso Ltd ✔ @casa_espresso ✉ @casa_espresso

Bradford's first speciality coffee roaster has a distinguished coffee background - despite roasting being a fairly recent development for the team.

Owner Nino Di Rienzo's dad was the original Sanremo UK distributor and it was Di Rienzo senior who, over a 15 year period, taught and inspired his son, who went on to create the new incarnation of the family business as a thriving artisan micro-roastery.

'OWNER NINO DI RIENZO'S DAD WAS THE ORIGINAL SANREMO UK DISTRIBUTOR'

Nino began roasting two years ago and with his small team of roaster Jonnie Drake and barista trainer Matthew Adams, has amassed an impressive number of customers.

The team uses a 5kg Probat to roast two seasonal espresso blends: Unione (a contemporary lighter roast with soft fruit and refreshing acidity), and the more

traditional Charlestown (rich dark chocolate and caramel notes). There's also a rotating seasonal single origin, *'we are constantly cupping and always keep it fresh and up-to-date with the new crops coming in,'* says Nino.

And the best bit about roasting? *'It's the feedback,'* he says. *'Sending out samples and getting enquiries from places we never thought we'd sell to.*

'With it being just the three of us, we can create very personal relationships with our customers through our interactions and the free training we offer,' he adds.

Ever expanding its reach, Casa Espresso is also bringing the Bradford roast to London outlets such as Lyle's and Store Street Espresso.

COFFEE BEANS AVAILABLE
SOLD ON SITE & ONLINE

COFFEE COURSES AVAILABLE

MAP 123. NORTH STAR COFFEE ROASTERS

Unit 33, The Boulevard, Leeds Dock, Leeds, West Yorkshire, LS10 1PZ.

www.northstarroast.com   T: 07725 144204

f North Star Coffee Roasters   🐦 @northstarroast   📷 @northstarroast

'**N**orth Star was established in 2013 as the first wholesale coffee roastery in Leeds,' says owner Holly Bowman. 'We're dedicated to providing coffee of the highest quality by working with speciality focused producers all over the world. That means we only buy speciality grade arabica coffees and choose beans based on their complex flavour profile, cleanliness and consistency.'

'HOLLY IS ONE OF JUST SIX FEMALE LICENCED Q GRADERS IN THE UK'

This year they've continued to break new ground, launching the North Star Coffee Academy in the city in March, to provide a wide range of accredited training courses for both the industry and the public.

Holly is one of just six female licenced Q graders in the UK, and was previously ethical coordinator and green buyer for Falcon Coffee. As a result, she has a great relationship with many farmers, although

North Star works with a variety of businesses who are bringing some of the best green beans from around the world to market.

As you'd expect, seasonality is key here, and beans are sourced in small quantities when they're at their best, before being roasted in small batches to showcase their inherent qualities.

So while one of its main espresso blends, Czar St (sweet and fruity) changes a few times a year in line with the coffee harvests, Dark Arches (caramel and chocolate) remains the same all year, although the flavour profiles of both stay fairly constant.

Check out the rotating menu of eight single origin coffees and its *'knockout'* organically processed decaf, too.

COFFEE BEANS AVAILABLE
SOLD ON SITE & ONLINE

COFFEE COURSES AVAILABLE

≥124. CIELO COFFEE ROASTERS

41 Main Street, Garforth, Leeds, West Yorkshire, LS25 1DS.
www.cielouk.com   T: 01132 863534

f Cielo Coffee   🐦 @cielouk   📷 @cielocoffee

Unlike other roaster-come-cafe combos, it was the coffee shop that came first at Cielo in Garforth.

Wanting to do business a little differently, Nick and Linda Castle opened the community space as a social enterprise in 2008 with the ambition to serve great quality coffee while supporting local people.

'Businesses often focus on either community values or quality products,' explains Nick, *'and we wanted to create somewhere which did both well.'* And what better way to control the quality of the speciality coffee served in your cafe than by taking the matter into your own hands?

"WE LOVE ROASTING RIGHT IN THE MIDDLE OF A COMMUNITY INSTEAD OF HIDDEN AWAY ON AN INDUSTRIAL ESTATE"

'Roasting the coffee ourselves not only gives us greater control of the character of the coffee,' says Nick, *'but it also enables us to find out more about the origins of the beans and support hard working farmers.'*

Setting up a roastery at its pioneering coffee house - you'll now find five Cielo cafes dotted around Leeds – roasters Linda and Hollie produce a number of seasonal blends, as well as a range of single origins from around the world on the Probat Probatone 5kg roaster. *'We love roasting right in the middle of a community instead of hidden away on an industrial estate,'* adds Linda.

Supplying its stable of Cielo cafes and - purely through word of mouth - a couple of local hangouts, Nick and Linda are now looking to expand their coffee empire in 2016 and stock cafes across the UK with Cielo's speciality beans.

COFFEE BEANS AVAILABLE
SOLD ON SITE & ONLINE

COFFEE COURSES AVAILABLE

125. DARK WOODS COFFEE

Holme Mills, West Slaithwaite Road, Marsden, Huddersfield, West Yorkshire, HD7 6LS.
www.darkwoodscoffee.co.uk   T: 01484 843141

f Dark Woods Coffee 🐦 @darkwoodscoffee 📧 @darkwoodscoffee

Dark Woods is the result of the meeting of three coffee professionals who found themselves living in the same beautiful corner of West Yorkshire.

Damian Blackburn has spent more than a decade roasting and sourcing beans, as well as travelling the world as a Cup of Excellence judge on a number of occasions. He encountered Paul Meikle-Janney who was running Coffee Community, providing barista training and consultancy to many international coffee organisations.

'THE ETHIOPIAN COFFEE CEREMONY, WITH GREEN COFFEE ROASTED IN A HEAVY PAN, OVER AN OPEN FIRE'

They then met Ian Agnew who was fighting the corner for coffee farmers through a number of charities and ethical companies. And the rest is history.

Dark Woods is still in Marsden, and based in Holme Mills, a striking, renovated weaving mill on the banks of the River Colne.

At its heart is a lovingly refurbished 1950s Probat, a heritage roaster which turns the carefully sourced, high grade speciality beans into very special coffee.

With years of experience and a deeply-held respect for the communities which produce those beans, the Dark Woods team is well placed to offer support and advice. Training is a priority and it's no surprise that Paul has been instrumental in writing the barista qualifications for both SCAE and City and Guilds, as well as having been head judge at the World Latte Art Championships for many years.

Dark Woods roasts for Michelin-starred restaurants and award-winning cafes, but at heart it has a simple ethos. Paul says, '*each of us has experienced the sights, sounds and simplicity of the Ethiopian coffee ceremony, with green coffee roasted in a heavy pan over an open fire, and it's something we keep in mind when we roast our own speciality coffees.*

'*This is a craft, but it doesn't need to be complicated to get the very best results.*'

COFFEE BEANS AVAILABLE SOLD ON SITE & ONLINE

COFFEE COURSES AVAILABLE

MAP №126. GRUMPY MULE

Bewley's, The Roastery, Bent Ley Road, Meltham, Holmfirth, West Yorkshire, HD9 4EP.
www.grumpymule.co.uk T: 01484 852601

f Grumpy Mule 🐦 @grumpymule 📷 @grumpy_mule

They may have been replaced by trucks, but mules were once the unsung heroes of the coffee trade, trekking great distances to carry the very best coffee cherries down the mountains.

Founded in 2006, Grumpy Mule is dedicated to supporting the really key people in the industry, using sustainable sourcing to ensure all of the growers enjoy a share of the success. The beans are then roasted with great care and precision to produce the finest flavours from the farmers' hard-earned harvest.

From one family to the next, Grumpy Mule was acquired by Bewley's in 2013, and now has a team with more than 20 years' roasting experience.

Two trusty Probat drum roasters, along with a Loring Smart roaster, allow the skilled roasters flexibility across batch size and roast profile to produce the best flavours from each coffee.

Long term relationships with a number of producers means that this West Yorkshire roastery often enjoys exclusive roasts – the prestigious Panama Esmeralda Special being a prime example.

As well as keeping cafe grinders across the country well stocked up, you'll also find Grumpy Mule's extensive range at delis, farm shops and other specialist food retailers across the UK.

COFFEE BEANS AVAILABLE ONLINE

COFFEE COURSES AVAILABLE

'THIS ROASTERY, NESTLED AMONG THE ROLLING HILLS OF THE HOLME VALLEY, IS THE HOME OF GRUMPY MULE. THIS IS WHERE THE MAGIC HAPPENS!'

127. HOPE & GLORY COFFEE CO.

Blenheim North, Elsham Wold Industrial Estate, Brigg, North Lincolnshire, DN20 0SP.
www.hopeandglorycoffee.co.uk T: 08009 890157

f Hope & Glory Coffee Co. @hopeandgloryuk @hopeandglorycoffee

From its little red roaster in Lincolnshire, Hope and Glory is on a mission to conquer the mail order coffee market.

Using super slim packaging that fits through the letter box for its coffee subscriptions, providing regular updates on the coffee, and recommending and selling domestic coffee kit, it's doing a great job of breaking down some of the speciality coffee geekery that frightens away newcomers.

Of course, all this would be pointless if it wasn't delivering a quality product in all senses of the word, so the skilled team of roasters are sourcing green beans from all parts of the coffee growing world - from El Salvador to Ethiopia.

It's not just the sourcing that they're acing either, as roastmaster Tommy's decades of experience means beans are roasted to perfection.

Its Blenheim Espresso Blend is the house special and best seller, while customers can also take a global gourmet getaway via an Around the World in Five Coffees selection or try the Ultimate Espresso Lover's Taster Pack. It also launched its first decaf this year, the Peruvian Cajamarca Swiss Water.

COFFEE BEANS AVAILABLE ONLINE

'BREAKING DOWN THE SPECIALITY COFFEE GEEKERY THAT FRIGHTENS AWAY NEWCOMERS'

Everything's roasted on a Monday in the 30kg Brambati, before being ground (or not) and packaged up to wing its way to make customers' breakfasts that bit more delightful the very same week.

MAP № 128. STOKES TEA AND COFFEE

Mint Lane, Lincoln, Lincolnshire, LN1 1UD.
www.stokes-coffee.co.uk   T: 01522 523548

f Stokes Coffee   🐦 @stokescoffee   ✉ @stokescoffee

The Stokes' story started in 1902 when founder Robert Stokes took over a Lincoln grocer's shop and began stocking the finest coffees and teas.

'STOKES IS LOOKING FORWARD TO EXPANDING WITH THE ADDITION OF A TRAINING CENTRE, CUPPING LAB AND COFFEE MUSEUM'

Four generations later and the family business now roasts speciality coffee on environmentally friendly Loring 35kg and 70kg roasters - previously using vintage models- taking the finest beans that have been carefully sourced to create award-winning coffee blends, such as its best-selling Blue Mountain Blend, created more than 50 years ago to emulate the smooth taste of Pure Jamaican Blue Mountain.

Working in partnership with Sanremo, Stokes helps businesses with everything from installing and maintaining coffee equipment to full barista training. It also offers a bespoke private label service to allow companies to create their own unique coffee branding.

Acquiring a former asylum, Stokes is looking forward to expanding with the addition of a training centre, cupping lab and coffee museum later this year.

But if you're just a regular Joe, looking for something to make your own cup of Joe, Stokes' online shop is the place to visit to stock up on supplies - from the comfort of your sofa.

COFFEE BEANS AVAILABLE
SOLD ON SITE & ONLINE

COFFEE COURSES AVAILABLE

MAP 129. NORTH STAR COFFEE ACADEMY

Unit 33, The Boulevard, Leeds Dock, Leeds, West Yorkshire, LS10 1PZ.
www.northstarroast.com   T: 07725 144204

f North Star Coffee Roasters   🐦 @northstarroast   📷 @northstarroast

North Star Coffee Academy is a fresh new addition to this year's guide. It launched in spring 2016, with the aims of sharing knowledge and promoting education about speciality coffee.

'It's the only purpose-built coffee training facility offering an extensive range of comprehensive courses between Scotland and London,' says Holly Bowman who also runs Leeds' North Star Coffee Roasters with Alex Kragiopoulos.

Holly is a licensed Q grader and SCAE authorised trainer, and is assisted in the new venture by SCAE professional barista and authorised trainer, Ollie Sears.

If that all sounds rather highfalutin, it's worth mentioning that this is a friendly and approachable team, who, in addition to running comprehensive courses for industry pros and the public on barista, brewing and sensory skills, will also design a bespoke course to suit customers' requirements and skill level.

And in addition to full courses, everyone's invited to go along to one of Hols and Ollie's monthly events which will include cupping sessions and industry talks. Keep an eye on the website and social media to find out what's coming up.

COFFEE BEANS AVAILABLE
SOLD ON SITE & ONLINE

COFFEE COURSES AVAILABLE

'"IT'S THE ONLY PURPOSE-BUILT COFFEE TRAINING FACILITY OFFERING AN EXTENSIVE RANGE OF COMPREHENSIVE COURSES BETWEEN SCOTLAND AND LONDON," SAYS HOLLY'

130. ARTEMIS COLD BREW COFFEE

Womersley, Yorkshire, DN6 9BB.
www.artemisbrew.co.uk   T: 07813 911414

f Artemis Brew   ✆ @artemisbrew   ◉ @artemisbrew

A passion for experimentation and a love of speciality coffee are the secret ingredients behind Ben Barker's coffee company which is devoted entirely to cold brew. And after three years perfecting his creation at home, he was finally ready to launch Artemis Cold Brew in 2015.

'COLD BREW COFFEE WATERMELON? YEP, REALLY'

If you're not down with it, here's the cold brew 101: it's made from freshly roasted coffee, slow brewed for 16 hours in filtered cold water to create a refreshing, less bitter, cold caffeine hit that's best served over ice.

It's a painstaking process which Ben has perfected to enable him to supply it both bottled, and nitro kegged (where it comes out looking rather like a glass of Guinness) to a host of coffee shops and bars. In selected speciality spots you'll find it used

The brew is best described as bright, clean and fruity with a bold acidity.

SOLD ON SITE
& ONLINE

'We mainly use an Ethiopian natural from Yirgacheffe,' Ben adds. *'It has the wow factor that helps differentiate cold brew from regular iced coffee. I've yet to cold brew a coffee we like more.'*

And because the bottles have a shelf life of 8-10 months, you can stock up and take them with you, wherever you are. *'We're always looking for new stockists,'* adds Ben. *'So give us a mention at your local coffee spot if we're not already there.'*

A growing band of coffee shops across the North are stocking Artemis – check the online stockist list – and you can buy direct from the website, too.

Also look out for the Artemis team at food festivals where you'll find them rustling up new cold brew experiences. Cold brew

MORE GOOD
ROASTERS

The North is full of beans ...

MAP 131.
COLOUR COFFEE
19 Goldspink Lane, Sandyford,
Newcastle upon Tyne, NE1 5DW.

www.colourcoffee.bigcartel.com

f Colour Coffee Roastery
w @colourcoffee
@ @colourcoffee

MAP 132.
PUMPHREYS COFFEE
Bridge Street, Blaydon upon Tyne,
NE21 4JJ.

www.pumphreys-coffee.co.uk

T: 01914 144510

f Pumphrey's Coffee
w @pumphreyscoffee
@ @pumphreyscoffee

MAP 133.
BEAN MILES
Wetheral, Carlisle, Cumbria, CA4 8LD.

www.beanmiles.co.uk

T: 07836 686870

w @beanmiles

MAP 134.
MR DUFFINS COFFEE
The Coffee Den, Kentmere Mills,
Silver Street, Staveley, LA8 9QR.

www.mrduffinscoffee.com

T: 01539 822866

f Mr Duffins Coffee
w @mrduffins
@ @mr.duffins.coffee

MAP 135.
TANK COFFEE
Unit 1, Acorn Business Centre, Leigh,
Greater Manchester, WN7 3DD.

www.tankcoffee.com

T: 0845 5570504

f Tankcoffee
w @tankcoffee
@ @tankcoffee

MAP 136.
MANCOCO
Arch 84, Hewitt Street, Manchester,
M15 4GB.
www.mancoco.co.uk

T: 01612 371916

f ManCoCo
w @mancocoltd
@ @mancocoltd

137.

SPECTRUM COFFEE ROASTERS

20j Evans Business Park,
Marston Moor Business Park,
Tockwith, North Yorkshire, YO26 7QF.

www.spectrumcoffeeroasters.co.uk

T: 07940175582

f Spectrum Coffee Roasters
y @spectrum_york
@ @spectrumcoffeeyork

138.

INDY COFFEE ROASTERS

Glyde House, Bradford, BD5 0BQ.

www.indyroasters.co.uk

T: 07702 920998

f Indy Coffee Roasters
y @indyroasters

139.

PUMP N GRIND

Leeds Innovation Centre,
103 Clarendon Road, Leeds, LS2 9DF.

www.pumpngrind.co.uk

f Pump n' Grind
y @pumpngrind
@ @pump.n.grind

140.

MAUDE COFFEE ROASTERS

82-83 Railway Street, Leeds,
West Yorkshire, LS9 8HB.

www.maudecoffee.co.uk

f Maude Coffee Roasters
y @maudecoffee
@ @maudecoffee

141.

FOUNDRY COFFEE ROASTERS

The Old Coach House, 9a Nether Edge
Road, Sheffield, S7 1RU.

www.foundrycoffeeroasters.com

T: 01142 509796

f Foundry Coffee Roasters Limited
y @foundrycoffee1
@ @foundrycoffeeroasters

142.

THE FORGE COFFEE ROASTERS

Don Road, Sheffield, S9 2TF.

www.forgecoffeeroasters.co.uk

T: 01142 441361

f Forge Coffee Roasters
y @forgeroasters
@ @forgecoffeeroasters

143.

SMITH STREET COFFEE ROASTERS

49 St Joseph's Road, Handsworth,
Sheffield, S13 9AU.

www.smithstreetcoffeeroasters.co.uk

T: 07915 091660

f Smith Street Coffee Roasters
y @smithstcoffee
@ @smithstcoffee

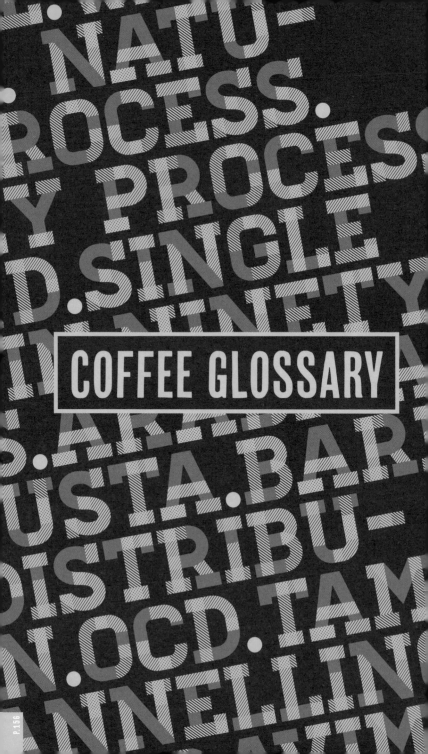

COFFEE GLOSSARY

ESPRESSO

BARISTA
The multi-skilled pro making your delicious coffee drinks.

CHANNELING
When a small hole or crack in the coffee bed of espresso forms, resulting in the water bypassing the majority of the ground coffee.

DISTRIBUTION
The action of distributing coffee evenly inside the espresso basket before tamping to encourage even extraction. This can be achieved through tapping, shaking or smoothing the coffee out with your fingers.

DOSE
The amount of ground coffee used when preparing a coffee.

GOD-SHOT
The name given to a shot of espresso when all the variables are in line and the coffee tastes at its optimum.

GRAVIMETRIC
The term for an espresso machine with the technology to control the yield, based on coffee dose.

OCD
Tool used for distributing coffee inside the espresso.

PRESSURE PROFILING
The act of controlling the amount of pressure applied to espresso throughout the extraction time, resulting in different espresso flavours and styles.

ROSETTA
The name given to the fern-like latte art pattern served on the top of a flat white or other milk drink.

TAMP
The action of compacting coffee into the espresso basket with a tamper in order to encourage even extraction.

YIELD
The volume of liquid produced when preparing an espresso or brewed coffee. A traditional espresso would yield twice that of the coffee dose. For example if you use 18g of coffee to brew an espresso, then you might yield 36g of liquid.

FILTER

AGITATE

Stirring the coffee throughout the brew cycle when preparing filter coffee to increase strength or encourage even extraction.

BATCH BREW

Filter coffee prepared on a large scale using a filter coffee machine.

BLOOM

The action of pouring water on freshly ground coffee to evenly coat each coffee particle. This encourages even extraction.

BREW

The general term given to filter coffee – as opposed to espresso.

CASCARA

The outer skin of the coffee cherry can be used to make an infusion served hot like a tea or cold, mixed with sparkling water.

COFFEE BLOSSOM

The flowers collected from the coffee bush are dried and can be used to make a tea-like infusion.

COLD BREW

Coffee brewed using cold water and left to extract over a longer period. Served cold, this coffee has high sweetness and low acidity.

CUPPING

The international method used to assess coffee. The beans are ground to a coarse consistency and steeped in a bowl of hot water for four minutes before the crust of grounds is scraped away from the surface. The coffee is left to cool and assessed via a big slurp from a cupping spoon.

EK43

Popular grinder used for both espresso and filter.

BEANS

ARABICA

The species of coffee commonly associated with speciality coffee, arabica is a delicate species which grows at high altitudes. It has lower levels of caffeine and typically higher perceived acidity, sweetness and a cleaner body.

BLEND

A blend of coffee from different farms and origins, traditionally used for espresso.

HONEY PROCESS

This process sits in-between washed and natural. The seeds are removed from the cherry and then left to dry with the mucilage intact, resulting in a sweet coffee with some characteristics of washed and natural process coffee.

NATURAL PROCESS

Naturally processed coffee is picked from the coffee bush and left to rest for a period of time with the fruit of the coffee cherry intact. In some cases the cherry can be left like this for two weeks before being hulled off. This results in a fruity, full body.

NINETY PLUS

All coffee is graded before sale with points out of 100. Speciality coffee will have 80 or more points. A coffee with 90 or more points is referred to as 90+ and will usually be quite exclusive, very tasty and expensive!

ROBUSTA

A low grade species of coffee, robusta grows at lower altitudes. This species has a high caffeine content and displays more bitterness and earthy flavours.

SINGLE ORIGIN

The term usually used for coffee from one origin. Single estate is the term used for coffee from one farm. Can be used for espresso or filter.

WASHED

Washed coffee is picked from the coffee bush and the outer layers of the cherry are immediately removed from the seed (what you normally call the coffee bean) and put into fermentation tanks to remove the layer of sticky mucilage before being laid out to dry. This washing process removes some of the sugars and bitterness so the coffee should have a higher acidity and lighter body.

Hannah Davies

'A COFFEE WITH 90 OR MORE POINTS WILL USUALLY BE QUITE EXCLUSIVE, TASTY AND EXPENSIVE!'

INDEX

	ENTRY NO		ENTRY NO
1901 Caffe Bistro	**73**	Coffee Genius	**8**
92 Degrees Coffee	**22**	Coffeekabin, The	**62**
Adams + Russell Coffee Roasters	**116**	Coffeevolution	**61**
Ancoats Coffee Co. – cafe	**25**	Colour Coffee	**131**
Ancoats Coffee Co. – roastery	**118**	Crosby Coffee	**113**
Anchor Coffee House, The	**88**	Dark Woods Coffee	**125**
Arch Sixteen Cafe	**76**	Depot Bakery, The	**64**
Artemis Cold Brew Coffee	**130**	Emily's By De Luca Boutique	**95**
Attic and Cafe Harlequin, The	**39**	Exchange Coffee Company – Clitheroe	**14**
Baltzersen's	**44**	Exchange Coffee Company – Blackburn	**15**
Barista's Coffee Co., The	**82**	Exchange Coffee Company – Blackburn Market	**79**
Bean and Bud	**43**	Exchange Coffee Company – Skipton	**93**
Bean Loved Coffee Bar	**47**	Exchange Coffee Company – Todmorden	**94**
Bean Miles	**133**	Exchange Coffee Company – roastery	**111**
Bedford St Coffee	**6**	Ezra & Gil	**85**
BLK Coffee	**1**	Farrer's	**108**
Bold Street Coffee	**21**	Federal Cafe & Bar	**29**
Bowery	**49**	Fenwick Foodhall	**4**
Bragazzis	**102**	Fig + Sparrow	**27**
Brew & Brownie	**38**	Flat Caps Coffee	**3**
Bristly Hog Coffee House, The	**10**	Flat White Cafe	**77**
Bunker Coffee & Kitchen	**74**	Flat White Kitchen	**5**
Cafe 164	**52**	Forge Bakehouse	**69**
Caffè & Co.	**18**	Forge Coffee Roasters, The	**142**
Caffeine and Co	**34**	Fossgate Social, The	**40**
Cartmel Coffee	**11**	Foundation Coffee House	**84**
Carvetii Coffee	**106**	Foundry Coffee Roasters	**141**
Casa Espresso	**122**	Grindsmith Espresso & Brewbar	**32**
Cedarwood Coffee Company	**17**	Grindsmith Media City	**33**
Cielo – Duncan Street	**54**	Grindsmith Pod	**30**
Cielo – Garforth	**60**	Grumpy Mule	**126**
Cielo – Crossgates	**99**	Hall, The	**12**
Cielo – Express Bar	**100**	Ham and Jam Coffee Shop	**16**
Cielo Coffee Roasters	**124**	Handmade Bakery, The	**63**
Coffee & Fandisha	**81**	Harvest	**2**
Coffee Aroma	**71**	Heart and Graft Coffee Roastery	**117**
Coffee Fix	**35**	Hedgerow, The	**46**

	ENTRY NO		ENTRY NO
Homeground Coffee + Kitchen	9	Pump n Grind	139
Hope & Glory Coffee Co.	127	Pumphreys Coffee	132
House of Koko	51	Red Bank Coffee Roasters	107
Hoxton North	45	Rinaldo's Speciality Coffee & Tea	109
Idle Hands	86	Roast Coffee & Kitchen	80
Indy Coffee Roasters	138	Roberts & Co.	112
J. Atkinson & Co.	110	Roost Coffee & Roastery	120
Joe Black Coffee	114	Root Coffee	20
Junction Coffee	23	Rounton Coffee	119
Kapow! Coffee	53	Smith Street Coffee Roasters	143
La Bottega Milanese	56	Sociable Folk	96
La Bottega Milanese – The Light	97	Spectrum Coffee Roasters	137
Laynes Espresso	57	Spring Espresso	41
Luckie Beans	103	Stanley & Ramona	92
ManCoCo – cafe	87	Steam Yard Coffee Co.	101
ManCoCo – roastery	136	Stokes Collection Cafe	70
Market House Coffee	36	Stokes High Bridge Cafe	72
Marmadukes Cafe Deli	67	Stokes Tea and Coffee	128
Maude Coffee Roasters	140	Takk Coffee House	26
Mint Hobo	7	Tamper Coffee – Sellers Wheel	68
Mr Duffins Coffee	134	Tamper Coffee – Westfield Terrace	66
Mrs Atha's	98	Tandem Coffee House	90
Music Room, The	13	Tank Coffee	135
Neighbourhood Coffee	115	Tea Hive	89
North Star Coffee Academy	129	Teacup Kitchen	28
North Star Coffee Roasters	123	Toast House	48
North Tea Power	83	Tynemouth Coffee Company	104
Opposite	55	Upshot Espresso	65
Opposite – Chapel Allerton	50	Westmoreland Coffee	42
Ouseburn Coffee Co.	105	Wolfhouse Kitchen, The	78
Out Of The Woods	58	Yay Coffee!	37
Out Of The Woods – Water Lane	59	York Coffee Emporium	121
Panna	19		
Perky Peacock, The	91		
Pink Lane Coffee	75		
Pot Kettle Black	31		
Providero	24		

COFFEE NOTES

Somewhere to save details of specific brews and beans you've enjoyed

COFFEE
NOTES

CITY CENTRE MAPS

Newcastle   168
Liverpool   169
Manchester   170
York   171
Leeds   172
Sheffield   173

NORTH OF ENGLAND MAP   175

Includes all entries not
on a city map.

COFFEE VENUE

ROASTER

MORE GOOD CUPS

MORE GOOD ROASTERS

All locations shown are approximate.

NEWCASTLE

Cafes

● BLK Coffee		1
● Harvest		2
● Flat Caps Coffee		3
● Fenwick Foodhall		4

Roasters

● Ouseburn Coffee Co.		105

More good cups

● 1901 Caffe Bistro		73
● Bunker Coffee & Kitchen		74
● Pink Lane Coffee		75
● Arch Sixteen Cafe		76

More good roasters

● Colour Coffee		131

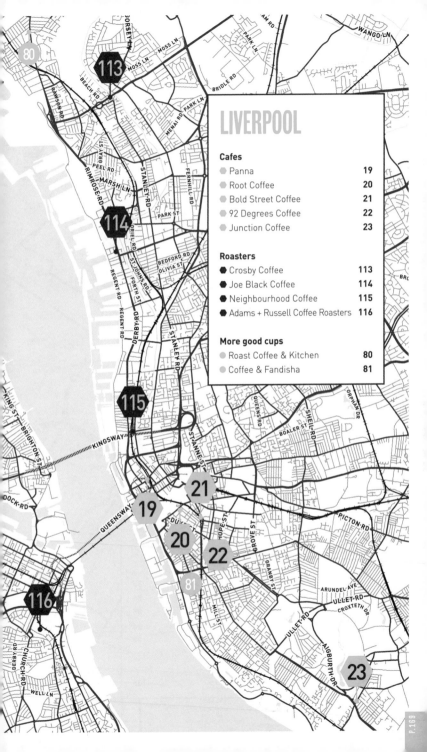

LIVERPOOL

Cafes

Panna	19
Root Coffee	20
Bold Street Coffee	21
92 Degrees Coffee	22
Junction Coffee	23

Roasters

Crosby Coffee	113
Joe Black Coffee	114
Neighbourhood Coffee	115
Adams + Russell Coffee Roasters	116

More good cups

| Roast Coffee & Kitchen | 80 |
| Coffee & Fandisha | 81 |

MANCHESTER

Cafes

Ancoats Coffee Co.	25
Takk Coffee House	26
Fig + Sparrow	27
Teacup Kitchen	28
Federal Cafe & Bar	29
Grindsmith Pod	30
Pot Kettle Black	31
Grindsmith Espresso & Brewbar	32

Roasters

Heart and Graft Coffee Roastery	117
Ancoats Coffee Co.	118

More good cups

North Tea Power	83
Foundation Coffee House	84
Ezra & Gil	85
Idle Hands	86
ManCoCo	87

More good roasters

ManCoCo	136

YORK

Cafes
- Brew & Brownie — 38
- Attic and Cafe Harlequin, The — 39
- Fossgate Social, The — 40
- Spring Espresso — 41

More good cups
- Perky Peacock, The — 91
- Stanley & Ramona — 92

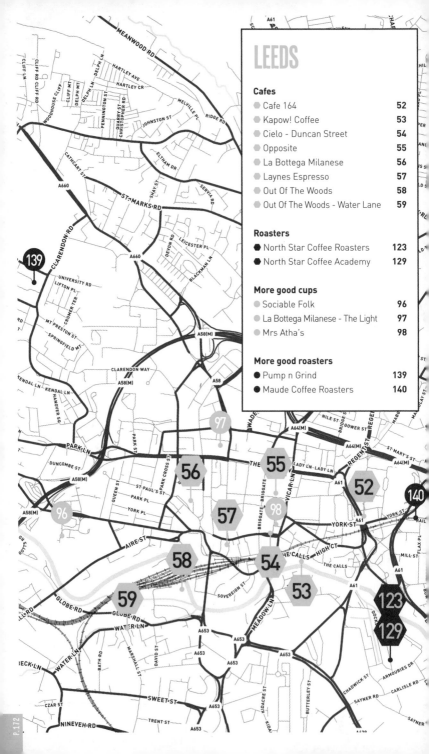

LEEDS

Cafes

- Cafe 164   **52**
- Kapow! Coffee   **53**
- Cielo - Duncan Street   **54**
- Opposite   **55**
- La Bottega Milanese   **56**
- Laynes Espresso   **57**
- Out Of The Woods   **58**
- Out Of The Woods - Water Lane   **59**

Roasters

- North Star Coffee Roasters   **123**
- North Star Coffee Academy   **129**

More good cups

- Sociable Folk   **96**
- La Bottega Milanese - The Light   **97**
- Mrs Atha's   **98**

More good roasters

- Pump n Grind   **139**
- Maude Coffee Roasters   **140**

SHEFFIELD

Cafes

- Depot Bakery, The — **64**
- Upshot Espresso — **65**
- Tamper Coffee: Westfield Terrace — **66**
- Marmadukes Cafe Deli — **67**
- Tamper Coffee: Sellers Wheel — **68**
- Forge Bakehouse — **69**

More good cups

- Steam Yard Coffee Co. — **101**
- Bragazzis — **102**

More good roaster

- Foundry Coffee Roasters — **141**

ROASTERS

Luckie Beans 103

Tynemouth Coffee Company 104

Carvetii Coffee 106

Red Bank Coffee Roasters 107

Farrer's 108

Rinaldo's Speciality Coffee & Tea 109

J. Atkinson & Co. 110

Exchange Coffee Company 111

Roberts & Co. 112

Rounton Coffee 119

Roost Coffee & Roastery 120

York Coffee Emporium 121

Casa Espresso 122

Dark Woods Coffee 125

Grumpy Mule 126

Hope & Glory Coffee Co. 127

Stokes Tea and Coffee 128

Artemis Cold Brew Coffee 130

MORE GOOD CUPS

Flat White Cafe 7?

Wolfhouse Kitchen, The 7?

Exchange Coffee Company – Blackburn Market 7?

Barista's Coffee Co., The 8?

Anchor Coffee House, The 8?

Tea Hive 8?

Tandem Coffee House 9?

Exchange Coffee Company – Skipton 9?

Emily's By De Luca Boutique 9?

Cielo Coffee – Crossgates 9?

Cielo Coffee – Express Bar 100

MORE GOOD ROASTERS

Pumphreys Coffee 13?

Bean Miles 13?

Mr Duffins Coffee 134

Tank Coffee 135

Indy Coffee Roasters 13?

Forge Coffee Roasters, The 142

Smith Street Coffee Roasters 14?

COFFEE VENUE

ROASTER

MORE GOOD CUPS

MORE GOOD ROASTERS

All locations are approximate.

CAFES

Flat White Kitchen	**5**
Bedford St Coffee	**6**
Mint Hobo	**7**
Coffee Genius	**8**
Homeground Coffee + Kitchen	**9**
Bristly Hog Coffee House, The	**10**
Cartmel Coffee	**11**
Hall, The	**12**
Music Room, The	**13**
Exchange Coffee Company – Clitheroe	**14**
Exchange Coffee Company – Blackburn	**15**
Ham and Jam Coffee Shop	**16**
Cedarwood Coffee Company	**17**
Caffè & Co.	**18**
Providero	**24**
Grindsmith Media City	**33**
Caffeine and Co	**34**
Coffee Fix	**35**
Market House Coffee	**36**
Yay Coffee!	**37**
Westmoreland Coffee	**42**
Bean and Bud	**43**
Baltzersen's	**44**
Hoxton North	**45**
Hedgerow, The	**46**
Bean Loved Coffee Bar	**47**
Toast House	**48**
Bowery	**49**
Opposite – Chapel Allerton	**50**
Cielo – Garforth	**60**
Coffeevolution	**61**
Coffeekabin, The	**62**
Handmade Bakery, The	**63**
Stokes Collection Cafe	**70**
Coffee Aroma	**71**
Stokes High Bridge Cafe	**72**

OPEN THE DOORS

TO A
WORLD OF
SPECIALITY
COFFEE

MEET OUR COMMITTEE

The *Northern Independent Coffee Guide*'s committee is made up of a small band of coffee experts and enthusiasts who've worked together with the rest of the coffee community to create this year's guide

DAVE OLEJNIK

Having always enjoyed working in and seeking out great coffee shops, it was during Dave's time living in Seattle (working as a touring guitar tech) that he was finally inspired to divert all his energies into his love of coffee. Back home, he worked for Coffee Community and went on to travel the world as a trainer and consultant, until eventually returning to Leeds to launch Laynes Espresso in 2011.

HANNAH DAVIES

Hannah's ten-year stint in the coffee industry has seen her grow from a barista in Liverpool to training manager and AST for a national coffee company. Hannah's current role as guild coordinator for SCAE allows her to fulfil her commitment to the coffee community in the UK and across Europe. In 2014, Hannah paired up with a fellow coffee lover and worked with the Manchester coffee scene to create Cup North – a coffee festival dedicated to showcasing the speciality coffee industry.

PAUL MEIKLE-JANNEY

After a career in catering in the UK and US, Paul began working in coffee in 1999 when he started his barista training and coffee consultancy, Coffee Community. Passionate about education, he helped write the City and Guilds barista qualification as well as those for the SCAE, and currently sits on the SCAE Education Committee (he's chair of its creators group). Paul co-founded Dark Woods Coffee Roasters in 2014 and has been involved in the World and UK Barista Championships from the start, as well as being head judge for the World Latte Art Championship and the World Coffee in Good Spirits Championship for four years. Other passions? DJing jazz and soul – and whisky.

IAN STEEL

Ian has enjoyed two careers – as a TV producer and a coffee roaster, both related, as they involve seeing ideas through from conception to completion. A vital part of his current job is telling the stories of farmers to the coffee drinking public.

By concentrating on quality and by investing – both locally and in initiatives at origin – his roastery, J. Atkinson and Co., aims to add value for both consumers and producers at either end of the supply chain.

NICK COOPER

Nick's day job is director at Salt Media, a boutique publishing and design company by the sea in Devon. His obsession with coffee started 15 years ago when he was living and working in Sydney. A couple of barista courses and a lot of flat whites later, he and his wife Jo returned to the UK to open an Aussie style coffee shop. They ended up creating Salt Media instead – but at least he now gets to create coffee guides. This year Nick was a guest speaker at Re:co, the speciality coffee forum in Dublin.